D0323637

Henrietta Szold

Record of a Life

Photo by Ganan's Studio, Jerusalem

Henrietta Szold

Henrietta Szold

Record of a Life

by ROSE ZEITLIN

THE DIAL PRESS NEW YORK 1952

Library of Congress Catalog Card Number: 52-10092

ACKNOWLEDGMENTS

The Author wishes to acknowledge, with gratitude, the assistance of the following, in making materials available and in granting permission for use of excerpts therefrom:

Norman Bentwich, author of JEWISH YOUTH COMES HOME, published by Victor Gollancz, Ltd., London.

Esco Fund for Palestine, for material from PALESTINE—A STUDY OF JEWISH, ARAB AND BRITISH POLICIES, published by Yale University Press (1947).

Hadassah, the Women's Zionist Organization of America, and their publications: The Hadassah Bulletin, The Hadassah News Letter and The Hadassah Newsletter.

The Viking Press, New York, publishers of Marvin Lowenthal: HENRIETTA SZOLD: LIFE AND LETTERS (1942).

Youth Aliyah office in Jerusalem.

The Zionist Organization of America and their publications: The Maccabaean and The New Palestine.

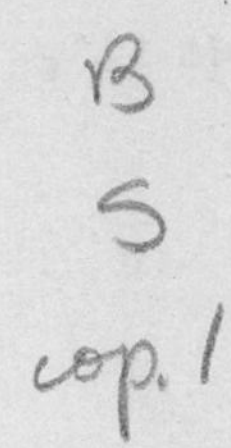

DESIGNED BY WILLIAM R. MEINHARDT

PRINTED IN THE UNITED STATES OF AMERICA BY

THE HADDON CRAFTSMEN, INC., SCRANTON, PENNA.

To the children—all eleven—of Henrietta's beloved nieces and nephews; and to my young Jonathan and David.

"It seems to me I have lived not one life, but several, each one bearing its own character and insignia."

Contents

Preface

IT IS to be regretted that Henrietta Szold did not write the story of her life. The principal reason for the omission was the fact that she was so completely absorbed in making the hours of each and every working day count that there were no moments left for setting down the record on paper. Four entries stand in a diary she once attempted to keep—entries that are tantalizing in what they reveal of humor, insight and pointed characterization.

To Zionists in general Henrietta Szold was known for the organizations and institutions she established one after another; those who had a closer view loved her for her broad humanity, and revered the independence and integrity of her mind. That independence of mind set her in opposition, at times, to official Zionist policy, especially where that policy touched educational principles or relations with the Palestinian Arabs. In the interest of objectivity, there has been no attempt, in this volume, to deny or to gloss over these differences between Henrietta Szold and the leadership of the Zionist Organization.

The record presented here is based on Miss Szold's letters, published and unpublished, on reports, articles, addresses, interviews with her friends and my own recollections. It does not pretend to be an exhaustive account of Miss Szold's life; its purpose is rather to give the reader some understanding of this rare and memorable personality.

Strict chronological order has not been followed. Miss Szold's activities were many and varied; each undertaking overlapped earlier work and was in turn overlapped by later tasks. For example, social welfare work, organized in Palestine in 1931 and continuing under her direction until 1939, was carried on simultaneously with the youth immigration work which began in 1933. These two activities were crossed by still other threads of work and other interests. Since rigid chronology would create confusion, it seemed desirable to arrange the material by subject matter, treating each subject as a unit.

For information supplementing the written records, and for much of the anecdotal material, I am indebted to many —in Palestine, to officials of Youth Aliyah headed by Hans Beyth, to leaders and teachers in settlements and children's villages, to more than eighty, in all, of Henrietta Szold's friends and co-workers. In particular I owe thanks to Dr. Julius Kleeberg, Miss Szold's personal physician; to Dr. Abraham Fuerst for his lucid and thoughtful exposition of the Child and Youth Foundation; to Sophia Mohl, whose home Henrietta shared for many years of her life in Palestine; and to Emma Ehrlich whose loving care of every item relating to Miss Szold has preserved much invaluable material. In New York, the Zionist Archives spared no pains in locating information and in checking data, and Dr. Joshua Bloch, Chief of the Jewish Division of the New York Public Library, was from first to last a tower of strength.

The expert editorial assistance received from Margaret Ladd Franklin smoothed out many rough spots in my text. To her I cannot sufficiently express my thanks, nor to those who read my script and gave me the benefit of their clarifying criticism and encouraging comments. Without such encouragement from Mrs. Edward Jacobs, past president of Hadassah, from Professor Joshua Neumann of Brooklyn College, from Dorothy Canfield Fisher, from Professor Allan Nevins of Columbia University, and others, it would have been difficult to pursue my path.

For similar assistance, as well as for the use of unpublished letters, I am likewise indebted to Bertha Szold Levin, Henrietta's surviving sister. The photographs used in this volume are reproduced by permission of the photographers, Ganan and Tim Gidal, and the courtesy of the national office of Hadassah.

R. Z.

Introduction

IT GIVES me pleasure to write a few words by way of introduction to Miss Zeitlin's book, because for me it has been a pleasure to read it. Upon a reader that did not know my sister Henrietta personally or know for what she stood as a Jewess and as a human being, the book cannot make the impression, I suppose, that it makes on me whose life was intertwined with hers in a sharing of influences and points of view. Even so objective a reader, however, must perceive that to her work Miss Zeitlin has brought the rich memories of a co-worker, intelligent, sympathetic understanding of the Zionist movement with which my sister's accomplishment was linked, familiarity with the Palestinian scene, scrupulous regard for accuracy and, finally, the devotion and loyalty of a friend.

Wherever Miss Zeitlin deals with matters about which as member of the family I may have more direct knowledge than others, I have checked the correctness of statements. The rest is well documented. Miss Zeitlin has had access to some unpublished material in this country and in Israel, and has been diligent in looking up printed sources and talking to friends and acquaintances of my sister. She has, I think, conveyed not only the significant outward aspects of her life, not only her obvious traits, but the true inwardness of her nature, not only what she did but what she was.

Miss Zeitlin set herself a difficult task, for in his own era an individual's importance can be as readily underestimated as overestimated. The subject of the book herself felt that her role in the welter of events that led to the establishment of a new state was a modest one, but historians cherish every contemporary record. From their point of view Miss Zeitlin has undoubtedly made a contribution to knowledge, and not merely written a tribute out of warmth of feeling.

BERTHA SZOLD LEVIN

Baltimore, February 6, 1952

Henrietta Szold

Record of a Life

1. *Baltimore*

"It is Lombard Street that makes for sympathy and understanding"

THE LITTLE stone house stood on the outskirts of Jerusalem, north of the Old City walls. Just off the road, it was set in a tree-planted garden, and from the six windows of her room her eye swept from east to south, then to west, on the sun-and-star-lit sky.

Across the Vale of Jehoshaphat to the east, Henrietta's eye sometimes continued its sweep, up along the noble ridge of Scopus and on to where the Mount of Olives, traditional burial place of Israel's hosts, raised row upon stark row of stone, unrelieved by green of grass, shrub or tree. Her thoughts slid back to the little gem of a burial place in her beloved Maryland, framed in tall hedge of Lombardy poplar, gracious with lawn and shade trees and bright shrubbery, where she longed to be laid, when her time came, near the dust of the father and mother she adored.

The roots of her family went back to Hungary, Rabbi Szold's forebears coming from the small village of Nemiskert where Benjamin, son of Baruch, was born in 1829, her mother's family, Schaar, from the neighborhood of Tyrnau. Both Szolds and Schaars were landowning families, the former tilling their own soil, the latter engaged in the brewing of beer. Family tales give a significant insight into the quality of the stock that produced Henrietta Szold. In one of her last letters home, Henrietta referred to the last will and testament of her grandfather, in which he directed that a certain field be sold to enable his son Benjamin to secure his rabbinical education. There was the story of the maternal grandmother, Miriam Loewenrosen Schaar, who took into her home two children of the local countryside, orphaned by the death of their parents, Catholic peasants of the neighborhood—orphans for whom no other door had been opened. And just as she engaged a Hebrew teacher for her own brood's religious instruction, so she brought into her home a Catholic priest for the proper training of the children she had so generously befriended. A family legend gave Miriam an ancestor out of medieval England, a prince of the blood royal, who fell so deeply in love with a Jewish maiden that he deserted his country and accepted Judaism for the sake of marriage with his beloved. Henrietta treated the story with scant respect. With even scanter respect, the mother disliked even hearing it mentioned. To both it appeared fanciful invention, an attempt to account for the family name of Loewenrosen (Lionrose).

Left a widow early, Miriam Schaar conducted the affairs of house and land. In her home she established a school for her own children, which the children of neighboring Jewish families also attended. Into this school Rabbi Benjamin Szold came as teacher. At the ripe age of fourteen the brilliant young scholar had been ordained, his degree giving him the right to decide questions of Jewish religious law, to perform marriages, to grant divorces. At eighteen he had stood on the barricades of Vienna and, after the abortive revolution, had been banished from the city. He had continued his studies, religious and secular, at Pressburg and at the University of Breslau, counting among his friends some of the most famous scholars of Europe. Introduced into the Schaar household as tutor, he fell in love with all of them. Blue-eyed Sophie, the youngest daughter, known in the village as *"die kluge Sophie"* (wise Sophie), became his bride.

Rabbi Szold's preaching in European pulpits had attracted attention, and the Jewish congregation of Stockholm, pleased by his voice, his personality and his presence, invited him to become its rabbi. At the same time an older colleague was invited to a post in Baltimore. Reluctant to transport his large family to that outpost of civilization, he suggested an exchange. With the consent of both congregations, Dr. Szold released the more desirable Stockholm position to his friend. In 1859 he and his wife Sophie settled in Baltimore. There, on December 21, 1860, Henrietta was born.

On the children who came after her—Rachel, Sadie, Bertha, Johanna, Adele*—Henrietta lavished the warmth of her loving nature. Her relationship with the younger ones was tinged with the maternal, and the parental influences filtered down to them through her. When Johanna, her darling, died at the age of three-and-a-half, Henrietta was so affected as to develop a serious nervous ailment. Adele, born the following year, became her special charge so that Bertha, then four, did not lose her place beside the mother at table, usually the prerogative of the youngest. Neither Bertha nor Adele remembered a time when Henrietta was not accepted by the elders as full equal.

Henrietta was thirteen when the family left its house in South Eutaw Street for the three-story brick building on Lombard Street that was to be its home for the next twenty years. Even moving day with its commotions and confusions had its sentimental associations. The children

* Estella and Rebecca had died in early infancy.

and the household goods were ready for transportation when it was suddenly realized that Rabbi Szold was nowhere about. Goods and family were compelled to leave without him. When they reached the new home, there was the Rabbi, in his own backyard, digging into the soil, planting his vine and his fig tree. Again and again Henrietta reverted to Lombard Street and its meaning in her life. "It is Lombard Street," she wrote from Jerusalem, "that makes for sympathy and understanding; the rest may do its worst or best—it won't eliminate that."

Books, music, handwork—Henrietta's darning was art and the tatting bobbin in her fingers fairly flew—filled the busy hours. Keeping the house supplied with fresh flowers was one of her special tasks, as was the dawn visit to the farmers' market for the daily stock of fresh garden produce. For the early riser she always was, this presented no hardship. The neighbor who tried to emulate the young Henrietta managed to get out of his gate in the morning in good time to meet her returning, a little negro boy trudging along at her side, carrying the big market basket laden with fruit and vegetables.

The emergency responsibilities arising in any household were, as of right, assumed by Henrietta. There were long weeks of quarantine with Adele during a siege of scarlet fever, days of nursing Bertha through an attack of diphtheria. "Kamelchen," her mother called her, "Little Camel," so matter of course was it for her to assume burdens.

In the Rabbi's study the eager mind of the daughter found the great formative influence of her life. Patterns of thought and feeling there took shape that molded the channel through which the stream of her life was to run. Though both were especially steeped in the study of Jewish history, poetry, ethics, and philosophy, the intellectual interests of father and daughter ranged through languages, literatures and histories ancient and modern. Dr. Szold could recite long passages from Homer by heart, and Henrietta, at the age of eight, was reading *Hermann und Dorothea.* Classic and modern philosophy formed part of their equipment—whatever, in short, constitutes ideal humanistic education, not divorced from, but related to the ordinary needs of ordinary human beings.

To judge from the portrait that hung in his daughter's New York apartment, Dr. Szold might have sat for a head of Tennyson, so like was the cast of countenance. Those who remember him testify to a grace and beauty of person matched by his charm, wisdom and rare humanity. Decades later a friend of those days recalled to Henrietta the "picture of that dear old man, sitting in his armchair, with a book not far away, talking in his charming, witty way about this and that, and throwing out bits of *Torah* (Law) and *Chochmah* (wisdom) to the delight of us all. A rare figure! We do not see that type in this world of tears and jazz and unrest."

Pupil and fellow-scholar, Henrietta became her father's amanuensis, assigned to numerous tasks of correspondence which had to meet exacting standards of form and content. *Aus der Fuelle,* was the injunction laid upon her, an expression that may be freely rendered, *out of the abundance of the heart.* Her heed of the injunction accounts perhaps for the fact that thousands of her letters are extant, treasured by their possessors.

Gardening and botanizing were delights shared by all the household from the Rabbi down. Her last home, in Jerusalem, was a bower, every plant cared for daily, and while her eyes served her, every chauffeur who drove her back and forth over the roads of Palestine knew he could count on stopping and starting a half dozen times while

Miss Szold clambered out of the car and up or down a scraggy hillside to identify some thorny growth or unexpected blossom, and expatiate to her companion on the amazing variety and beauty of Palestine's flora, even during the rainless, unpromising summer months.

High standards of conduct, adherence to religious form and ritual—throughout her life Miss Szold was an observant Jewess—did not mean an atmosphere of stern and unbending discipline. Five growing girls filled the house with activity and laughter. Serious intellectual pursuits had their counterbalance in walks in the Maryland woods, in gardening, in household tasks, in out-and-out frivolities. A long button-chain strung through the front hall received passionate attention; hours upon hours were spent in silly name-games.

Relatives and friends coming from a distance had sometimes to be accommodated for long periods with bed and board. Babies were bedded the summer long on the ample top of the large square piano. But in a Rabbi's home family life could never be completely personal. Congregational duties, community interests, and the world's cruelties brought visitors galore. Henrietta and her father were on the docks in Baltimore when the ships came in, and the Czar's victims had the comfort of welcoming hands and a well-stocked table in the Szold home.

A childish adventure, the subject of later reminiscences, left an indelible impression, not so much because of the adventure itself, as through its repercussions. The little girl of five had been hearing much talk in the house concerning the visit to Baltimore of the distinguished Polish actor, Bogumil Dawison, whose performances of the great roles of classic German drama were exciting the eastern seaboard. Fired by her parents' enthusiasm, she begged to be taken along to the theatre. Gravely her father told her that tickets were expensive, that he had already purchased two, and was not rich enough to buy any more. If she wished to visit the theatre she must have Herr Dawison's personal invitation. Gravely the child listened and, waiting until the Sabbath when she was dressed in her best, she slipped alone out of the house and inquired her way to Herr Dawison's hotel. Knocking at the door, she presented herself as the rabbi's daughter, not doubting that her father's fame would serve as adequate introduction. The little thing's engaging ways—her good German, too—must have gone straight to the great man's heart, for she was welcomed, made to feel completely at home, and returned to her parents with the coveted theatre tickets clutched in her hand.

The innocent exploit received publicity and the comments and exclamations that followed, the attentions showered on her, frightened the child and made her shrink from notice. To this incident she attributed her years of shyness and the torture that accompanied her appearance on a public platform—a feeling which disappeared only after her first visit to Palestine in 1909, when she and her mother conceived the idea that was to bear fruit in the achievements of the organization *Hadassah*.

Girlhood and young womanhood marked the beginnings of many lasting friendships. With many of the young men who flocked to the Szold home Henrietta was to maintain a correspondence through life. There was Fabian Franklin, mathematician and economist, later associate editor of *The New York Evening Post*; Harry Friedenwald, who became one of the country's most distinguished ophthalmologists; Joseph Jastrow, who was to win a name as one of America's foremost psychologists and who became her brother-in-law through marriage with Rachel, and Louis H. Levin, noted social worker who married Bertha.

In a now-it-may-be-told vein Adele,* youngest of the girls, once disclosed to friends that many of the frequent visitors to the Szold home came for the purpose of calling on the oldest daughter but, busy in her father's study, Henrietta passed on to the younger girls the pleasant duty of entertaining the callers.

For her early intellectual maturity, for the concentration of her interests on family and community, she was to pay a heavy price. "I have had a full and rich life," she said once, "not a happy one." Never did she cease regretting her childlessness. For much of her life she could not bear even to refer to it. One self-revelation in a letter of 1917 to Jessie Sampter, friend and co-worker on the Central Committee of Hadassah: "Deep down in the bottom of my heart I have always held that I should have had children, many children. It is only in rearing children that minute service piled on minute service counts. In my life details have confused the issue; they have not gone to make a harmonious and productive whole. In a mother's life, ability to lose one's identity in details is the great thing for the future of mankind." Late in life she confided freely to friends: "I would exchange everything for one child of my own."

In 1881, on a visit to Europe with her father, Henrietta busied herself with tracing the family in all its ramifications. She went to the villages where Szolds had lived and died, one of her interests being to trace the name to its origin. This she did not succeed in doing until after her arrival in Palestine in 1920 when a letter from a young *Halutz* (pioneer) of the name Sold cleared it up for her. The information bore out what had previously been only

* later Mrs. Thomas Seltzer

conjecture on her part. The name had been assumed by a forebear, Michael, the first Jew in Galicia to hold a salaried (*besoldeter*) position under the government. The root of the word formed the name. On the removal of one branch of the family to Hungary, in the middle of the century, the letter *z* had been introduced into the spelling in order to keep the original pronunciation.

Henrietta's sense of belonging to her father's and mother's people went almost to the extent of identification with them. To the aunt who met her at the railroad station, her greeting was: "My brown-eyed mother!"

The identification lasted through life. Near the end of her days, discussing with a committee of workers the foods to be stored for the relief of refugees, she objected vehemently to the inclusion of lentils. Pressed for her reason, she revealed the source of her aversion. According to the practice of her father's day, poor students at the rabbinical seminaries received their meals at the tables of the townsfolk. To spread both expense and privilege the student ate in a different home each day. "Poor fellow, he must be hungry," was the sympathetic thought of the housewife. "We'll cook lentils—that's properly filling." So from day to day the "poor fellow" ate his lentils. So properly lentil-fed was he that before his marriage Rabbi Szold exacted a solemn vow from his Sophie never to serve lentils on the Szold table. "I beg you," said Miss Szold to her friends, "no lentils." It may be said, parenthetically, that lentils did appear with due frequency on the Szold table.

One of the Rabbi's injunctions to his children was to have a central interest in life, but he warned them never to permit that central interest to become a single interest. Henrietta's interests were indeed varied, partly in response to her father's precept; partly, no doubt through the example of her mother, who could walk into a despairing hostess's kitchen and demonstrate to her the method of preparing *matza kloes* with the proper degree of lightness, or conduct a guest on a tour of the majolica collection in the Metropolitan Museum of Art, delivering on it a lecture worthy of the collection.

"My father's daughter said . . ." "my mother's daughter did . . ." were recurring phrases from Miss Szold's pen. She had inherited, so she declared, her mother's nature; her sense of the practical, her feeling for organization in the large and in detail, came from that source. But that inherited nature, she further explained, had been shaped and molded by the scholarly ideals, the deeply spiritual thought and feeling of the rabbi father.

In the main her sisters agreed with her. Said Bertha: "I might say that from our father she derived her broad charity, democracy, respect for learning, interest in large affairs, and tolerance for the ways of others, combined with the power of righteous indignation at injustice or meanness; from our mother, her sense for the practical with the energy to carry out the will, and the industry to make each minute of her time golden with worthwhile achievement; from both the counsel of perfection in whatever is undertaken."

To which Adele added: "The stern self-discipline she practised upon herself from childhood up cannot be accounted for by direct heredity or training or any human influence. Compared with her Dr. and Mrs. Szold were pagan hedonists." "Her earnestness was incapable of misinterpretation," she said at another time. "The lowest-minded could tell that her concern was not with priggish self-glorification; her sole aim was perfection in order to enthrone not herself, but perfection."

Writing to her sisters from Jerusalem on the anniversary of her father's death, Henrietta says: "Nineteen years ago! Out here my recollection of him, his views, and his attitude toward all sorts of questions has become more vivid rather than less. As problem after problem comes up —and life here bristles with them—I involuntarily ask myself how he would have met them; he seems to me a modern of moderns. At all events, summoning back to my mind his way of dealing with social human perplexities helps me to serenity better than anything else." Again: "Today was the twentieth anniversary of Papa's death. I cannot say I thought of him more today . . . for I think of him every day."

When Miss Szold arrived in Berlin in 1935 to discuss plans with the Jewish community in connection with youth immigration to Palestine, a surprise came that took her off her feet. Mr. Julius Seligsohn,* head of the Jewish community of Berlin, in introducing her, recalled to the assemblage an event of fifty-three years earlier—a commemoration service he had attended in Philadelphia for the hundredth birthday anniversary of Moses Mendelssohn. The main address had been delivered by Dr. Benjamin Szold. Mr. Seligsohn proceeded to quote striking passages from the address, the implication being that the daughter was the legitimate successor of a distinguished father. Consternation, embarrassment, pride, were the feelings aroused in the seventy-four-year-old woman. "Ever since I have been living in Palestine, I have had the feeling that I hadn't the protection of the rock from which I was hewn. And here suddenly the rock was the important feature. I confess I felt solemn and touched."

It was on Baltimore that her mind dwelt in her last years. To her friends in Jerusalem she said sadly: "I know

* Mr. Seligsohn came to the United States later to seek help for his co-religionists. Although he could have remained, he returned to Germany in order to help others escape. He died at Dachau.

every one here, but no one knows me because no one knows my background."

An octogenarian, celebrating her birthday with her staff about her, it was of those memories that she spoke, memories going back to Civil War days. "I was an infant," she told them. "My father set me on his shoulder and said: 'Look out. You will see them now, bearing Abraham Lincoln to his grave.' Then he told me about the man Lincoln."

The gift that went to her heart on that birthday came from Dr. Judah L. Magnes, President of the Hebrew University. Some time earlier she had presented to the University Library the manuscripts left by Dr. Szold. Unknown to her, Dr. Magnes had assigned to two students the task of studying the manuscripts. Now, as part of her birthday celebration, Dr. Magnes presented her with the essays in which the students had incorporated their findings. That gift, Miss Szold told him, brought her solace because it connected her with America, her home background. "You were the one," she continued, "who proclaimed my roots and my trunk and the sap that made me truly alive. And at the very end, the meeting with your students in your eyrie, let me feel the full worthwhileness of the past, seeing that my Palestinian branches had grown into the future." Then she went on to pay full meed of tribute to the mother whose careful outlay of household expenses had made possible the publication of the father's *Commentary on Job*. "There, too, lay a root of my being."

2. *Tradition*

"to know the exigencies of his time and be able to do battle with them"

IMMEDIATELY upon her graduation from the Western High School, Henrietta continued her academic career as a teacher. Teaching was not a new venture; she was already conducting classes in Hebrew, Jewish history and in the Bible in the religious school of her father's synagogue. A fairly short period of teaching at the Western High School was followed by an appointment at a private school run by three Baltimore ladies, the Misses Adams. Here, for fifteen years, Miss Henrietta, as she was called, taught at one time or another English, German, French, Latin, mathematics, history, botany, physiology—practically everything offered in the high school curriculum. An enumeration of these subjects, attributed to a present-day teacher, would constitute a charge of dilettantism. The suspicion cannot be entertained in her case for, as in everything she did, her grounding was sure. A white-haired lady, once her pupil, asserted plaintively: "I never learned mathematics because Miss Henrietta was not my teacher in that subject." Another testified feelingly that the greatest experience in her long life was her schoolgirl contact with Henrietta Szold.

At that time, in the 1870's, the Jewish population of the United States was not much more than 200,000. It consisted of two elements—Spanish Jews who, after their expulsion from Spain in 1492, had emigrated to England or Holland, thence to the United States; and German Jews, originally a forty percent minority, whose numbers increased considerably during the middle decades of the nineteenth century. The earlier group clung to its ancient rituals; the Germans were split into two religious camps —orthodox and reform. Dr. Szold upheld the traditions of the orthodox, but not in the fashion of the extremists who held to every jot and tittle of the law. His was the middle-of-the-road group that took on the name "conservative." In the 1880's and 1890's a new Jewish group, from Poland, Russia, and countries bordering on Russia produced a rapid increase in the Jewish population of the United States, making it one million by 1900. This third group of immigrants brought with it an avid interest in cultural pursuits, general and Jewish. It was with this third group that the Szolds felt close sympathy.

Before her seventeenth birthday Henrietta Szold was producing articles, under the pen-name *Sulamith,* for several English-Jewish periodicals, among them *The Jewish Messenger,* published in New York. Her column, *Our Baltimore Letter,* at first a bit stilted and over-elaborate in construction, soon took on ease and vigor. Her comments on American Jewish life expressed the writer's enthusiasms and condemnations, and always her emphasis was on the value of tradition. In particular she lashed out at what she called materialism, which she defined as devotion to the activities of business and pleasure to the neglect of cultural pursuits. The chord is struck repeatedly, as when she states that, judging by what appeared in the columns of the English-Jewish press, "Jewish life seems to consist entirely of Jewish betrothals, Jewish entertainments, Jewish balls and Jewish boasting, interlarded with a dose of caustic Jewish disputation and rabbinical sarcasm and, as the one good ingredient, Jewish charity." On being denounced for holding her people up to criticism, her reply came in forthright terms—that she denounced her people's shortcomings precisely because she had their welfare at heart. She warned her critics not to shrink from facts, but to examine and investigate, establish truth or falsity, and act accordingly. It was only in this way that they would command respect, and become a factor in society.

On occasion *Sulamith*'s shafts took more personal aim. Chafing at certain offensive references to both Jewish and Christian holiday observances, which had appeared in the pages of *The American Israelite,* Miss Szold attacked both writer and editor, charging them with breaches of good taste and of moral nicety. Affirming that every religious rite had some justification and that all religions, when truly adhered to, ennoble and refine, she protested that the columns of the journal should not be open to profanities and blasphemies. Her protest was answered with a jeer. She was hailed as "dear pot-and-pan scourer," and the offending writer further outraged her religious sensibilities by stating that "women's hearts and women's bonnets lead them to the house of prayer." Nothing loath, Sulamith proceeded to demolish both writer and editor. The editor "leaves it to his subordinates to occupy themselves with my antics, sustaining perfectly my charge of carelessness; the other [the writer] employs the most abusive epithets a man can apply to a woman, a proceeding which is usually called vulgarity; and both ridicule me on account of my sex, proof positive of the narrow-mindedness of which their thoughtless reform of Judaism is a part . . . Is telling me that I am a woman, nothing but a woman, a refutation of my charges? . . . My grammar may be below criticism, my English style execrable; all this I can readily admit; but is the *Israelite* for that reason any more Jewish, any more literary, or any less vulgar?" She admitted her inability to understand certain motives and actions, and hoped that vulgarity, disgusting manners, unrefined taste, puerile ridicule, sacrilege, and want of conscience would always remain below her comprehension.

It was characteristic of the young champion that her championship embraced alien religions as well as her own. "I would consider it almost a sin," she wrote, "to say one word against the Christmas festival; it opens so many hearts and tears them out of their self-absorption; friends are tied closer in the bonds of friendship; enemies are forgetful of hatred and animosity and join with zest in the pleasure of the season; the poor are remembered and amply provided for; not a household but has for its inmates joy and love on that day . . . Christmas truly fulfills its mission of bringing peace and good will to men."

Speaking before the Baltimore section of the National Council of Jewish Women, in 1896, Miss Szold declared the Law to be the blood of the race, the soul of the faith, the quickening force in Jewish life. To the vast, incomplete mosaic of systems, ideas, theories, fancies, poesy, romance and ethical principles, each generation had furnished builders, each nation had contributed vari-colored stones, and on each stone was stamped the inscription—the Law. She pointed to the miracle that despite persecution, homelessness, ostracism, and old age, the Jews had enriched every literature of Europe, besides adding to their own. She quoted the philosopher Mill: " 'If this be one-sidedness, it is the one-sidedness, the concentration of genius.' "

Again she said: "When we have ceased to be the efficient guardian of our treasures, of what use are we in the world?

I fear that in the case of such a flagrant dereliction of duty the twentieth century will have in store for us not a Ghetto, but a grave." The grave Miss Szold foresaw was assuredly not the physical grave of millions of slaughtered innocents. Her nineteenth century belief in the perfectibility of man would have forbidden the entertainment of that thought. What she dreaded was rather the spiritual grave of Judaism deserted by indifference and ignorance.

Her European travels in 1881 and 1909 confirmed and strengthened her convictions. The first trip, taken with her father, introduced her to the communities of Central Europe. In 1909, she was again in Europe, in company with her mother. After travel in England and on the continent, they turned east and visited the ancient centers of civilization—Constantinople, Smyrna, Alexandria, Beirut, Damascus, and finally, Jerusalem. Returning by way of Italy, they toured its museums, cathedrals, and churches. These monuments of Catholicism strengthened her conviction that loyalty to an idea, constancy in the realization of an ideal, were what counted in human history. In the cathedrals and in the Madonna cult Miss Szold found the same affirmation of tradition as in her own Judaism—"an attempt on the part of thousands to realize an ideal, and realize it so that every detail of its expression may testify to its reality."

Early and late this feeling for the spiritual values in tradition cropped up—in letters, in addresses, in articles in *The Jewish Messenger*, even in one of the otherwise objective articles which she contributed to *The Jewish Encyclopedia*. In her article on Grace Aguilar, Miss Szold accounted for her subject's depreciation of Jewish tradition by the fact of her Marano ancestry and her country life, cut off from association with Jews.

Her sense of the importance of cultural values led to

repeated emphasis on education, direct and indirect. As school teacher, problems of secular education concerned her. Long before the initiation of courses in pedagogy and the establishment of teachers' training schools, she was advocating principles that have since become a commonplace of pedagogy—the prime importance of newspaper study as a means of broadening the intelligence and sympathies; the true utility of emphasizing the elements which educate the man—whether he is to be carpenter, banker, shoemaker, hod-carrier, or college professor.

In the sphere of religious education Miss Szold felt that her people needed only to become acquainted with their own history in order to be aroused from lethargy in the sphere of religious thought, for history and religion were linked so closely that admiration for the one was bound to incite love for the other. She praised the Polish-Jewish congregation in her own Baltimore because, instead of putting young and inexperienced girls in charge, it was engaging men of learning to guide the children in the tenets of their faith. The Christian Sunday School idea, aped by Jewish congregations, she rejected as insubstantial: "Jewish youth must be initiated in the glories of our history and thus learn to know the shortcomings and exigencies of his own time, and be ready to do battle with them."

It was natural, in thinking of the future of Judaism, that Henrietta Szold should be concerned with the education of the Jewish girl who, through the home and her influence upon it, was the conserver of her people's tradition. She grieved over the breakdown of Jewish home life in America, and attributed it to the failure to educate Jewish girls, secularly and religiously. On the one hand, Jewish Reform, adopting the modern principle of education for girls, made the mistake of accepting a smattering of superficial knowledge. Orthodox groups, on the other hand, to whom tradition was spiritual mainstay, rejected the idea of modern education for their daughters. But the Jewish heart, Miss Szold maintained, starved unless fed through the Jewish intellect. When the late Dr. Samson Benderly, first secretary of the Jewish Education Association, set himself to the task of organizing the chaotic world of Jewish education in the United States, it was with Henrietta Szold that he worked out his program for school organization and teacher training.

It is not to be supposed that, in her emphasis on intellectual education for girls, Miss Szold intended to exclude or minimize the arts of home-making. On the contrary—as priestess of the home, the woman was the center of the Jewish family. Her defection in duties of religious observance and in the inculcation of belief in her children, was more serious than that of her brother would be. Much later, when recruiting forces for active Hadassah work, she frowned upon participation by mothers of young children in any activities which took them out of the home. Mrs. Blank, on the Board of Directors, had been delinquent in attendance at successive meetings of the Board. Regulations required that she be dropped from Board membership. "I understand that she has a young baby," says Miss Szold in excuse. "Oh, the baby isn't so young; it's nine months old," returns the accuser. "If I had a baby nine months old," counters Miss Szold, "nothing would get me to a meeting."

3. *Russian Immigration*

"I eat, drink and sleep Russians"

THE YEAR 1860 had seen the birth of two great-souled leaders in Zionist life—Theodor Herzl and Henrietta Szold. Superficially there was no parallel in the lives of the two great organizers. Theodor Herzl was born into an assimilationist home, spent his formative years in an environment alien to Jewish interest and, upon reaching man's estate, became a brilliant newspaper correspondent, at home in the intellectual circles of European capitals, marked off in no way from his colleagues other than by his magnetic personality, majestic presence and high-mindedness. Henrietta Szold, on the other hand, was born and bred in a home steeped in Jewish learning and tradition.

Nevertheless, without laboring the point too much, it may not be far-fetched to point out one significant parallel. Out of the shock of the Dreyfus trial, in 1894, Herzl's program of political Zionism was born. Only dimly aware of the existence of a movement Zionward, he evolved independently his concept of a Jewish state. East European Jewry, desperate, longing for emancipation and spurred by Leo Pinsker's *Auto-Emancipation,* already had its Lovers-of-Zion groups and had founded by this time a number of rural settlements in Palestine. Herzl's *Der Judenstaat* (*The Jewish State*), published in 1896, became the beacon for these groups, and its author was prevailed upon to call into being the first World Zionist Congress. Meeting in Basle in 1897, the Congress based its program on the organization of a world body dedicated to obtaining its objective, not by haphazard infiltration into Palestine, but through political action, the hoped-for channel being the Turkish government in whose empire Palestine lay, and Turkey's ally, the German Kaiser.

In 1893, four years before the world organization was founded, Henrietta Szold had joined the Zionist Association of Baltimore, the first organized Zionist group in the United States—a group which maintained its identity until it merged with the later-organized, national Federation of American Zionists. As in Herzl's case, it was a spiritual experience, the shattering experience of the Russian pogroms and her close personal contact with its victims fleeing into the then open refuge of the New World, which led her to embrace the new philosophy.

The Russians began coming into Baltimore after the pogroms of 1881, set off by the assassination of Czar Alexander II. (Though habitually referred to as Russians, they actually came, with few exceptions, from Poland, Lithuania and other parts of the Russian empire.) In the settled Jewish community of Baltimore, they created a ferment and a problem. Alien in speech and in appearance, they became mere objects of commiseration and of sporadic philanthropy to the Baltimore Jews of West European heritage, who, offended by superficial crudities, failed to penetrate to the inner spiritual core of the Easterners.

The intellectuals among the newcomers gravitated toward Rabbi Szold, in whose household they found warmth and understanding. Meeting on common ground, they organized a Hebrew Literary Society of which Miss

Szold and her father became active members. It was this society, small in numbers and weak in funds, that initiated the plan for practical activity in behalf of the immigrants, the plan taking the form of a night school for the teaching of English, American history and vocational subjects. We may be sure, even in the absence of direct evidence, that the spur to action came from the young schoolteacher, that hers was the guiding hand, setting up the program, planning the administrative details, and handling most of them as well.

The night classes were held in two rooms in a loft. The young men of the society, who contributed of their meager funds for the purchase of books, writing materials, and kerosene lamps, also sharpened pencils, washed slates, swept rooms, and painted floors. They let down the shutters and put them up night after night. Tuition fees were thirty cents a month. Teachers were engaged at $15 a month, and during the first semester six hundred and fifty adults were introduced to the complexities of the English language. Two years later an expected enrollment of two hundred and thirty-five pupils rose to three hundred and forty, a development unexpected and unprovided for, but met with characteristic energy by Miss Henrietta, the principal. By 1898, when the school was taken over by the city, five thousand pupils, Jewish and non-Jewish, had received instruction.

Letters written to Rachel Szold Jastrow, married and living in Madison, Wisconsin, reflect the energetic activity of the period. One letter records the activities, here given in outline form, of two days in November, 1891:

Monday—up at 5:30

6:30: Correspondence with teachers of the Russian school and others; telephone calls for substitute teachers [made from the corner drugstore as there was no telephone in the Szold home]; breakfast;

9—3: Teaching at the private school kept by the Misses Adams;

After 3: Shopping for books, pencils, etc., for two new classes organized because of unexpectedly large registration; meeting of Botany Club until 6; supper at home;

7: Russian school;

11:30: Home (no dinner that day).

Tuesday—Correspondence for Botany Club
Breakfast
School
Woman's Literary Club—hour's meeting of executive board
Daughters in Israel—speaking engagement
Supper
Russian school
Home—11:30 (no dinner that day).

Those who have worked with Henrietta Szold will recognize the record of activity, and wonder perhaps at the late rising hour of 5:30. The two-day record of crowded hours represents the customary current of her life down to its last four or five years, when she complained despairingly of having to slow down to a regimen of twelve hours daily, although to do what was required called for at least eighteen.

Even more forcibly than the activity, the letters reflect the influence exerted on her sensitive mind by the Russian Jewish immigrants. An ideal something she found in them inspired her, and her great wish was to be able to give them her whole strength, time and ability. The subject absorbed her so completely that she felt again her girlish longing to be a man so that she might mature plans of great benefit to them. "I eat, drink and sleep Russians," she wrote—and "The only thing I can talk about is the opening of the night school."

When the classes were in session, the organizers sometimes met for discussion. Many years later, in loving, sensitively phrased words, Miss Szold drew portraits of two of the organizers: "If *Daniel Deronda* had not been published at least ten years earlier, I should be tempted to believe that George Eliot had peeped into the chiaroscuro of the rooms on Front Street to find the local color for her 'Philosophers' club meetings. Her Mordecai was there, fervent, thoughtful, eloquent, nationally optimistic, and, alas, sick, sick unto death. And one was there whom she, even she with her insight into Jewish life, did not know, and could not have known. The 'colporteur' of hope was a product of the Herzlian Zionism that came along after her day. He was a dear old man, the only old man in the group . . . He said little, except what is expressed by the mildest and darkest of steady brown eyes, by resting heavy, horn-rimmed spectacles first on the forehead, and then on the very tip of a retroussé nose when the discussion waxed hot, or by letting a lean frame slip down on the chair until it sank almost out of sight. As he sat there with his arms crossed over each other at the wrists, he looked like Israel the martyr—his spirit was Israel the seer's."

In every comparison she makes between the new Jewish group and the old, the former comes out ahead because of its attachment to spiritual ideals, its courage and readiness to make sacrifices for intellectual advancement, while the others she sees vulgarized by prosperity. She is infuriated by a young lady who has gone back on her promise to teach on the plea that going out at night may injure her reputation, and by another who fails to report at school because she must attend a wedding.

It was this close association with the East Europeans, particularly with the intellectuals with whom she founded the night school, that made a Zionist of Henrietta. Adequate foundation for Zionism there had been through her growing years—her mother's home, her father's study, the prayer book, Jewish history. Now, to crystallize it all, came the Russians, re-enacting after nineteen centuries of dispersion, the oft-repeated experiences of her people.

The idea that a homeless people needed a home for the sake of its dignity and self-respect, for its own spiritual rehabilitation, even more than as a refuge for outcasts, was an idea so completely simple, so utterly logical, that it needed no argument. Zion was to be the refuge of the Jew. It was also to be the refuge of Judaism—Jewish Law was to be the Jewish way of life, Jewish ethics the Jewish rule of life. The writer recalls a categorical statement, made by Henrietta Szold many years ago. She would feel compelled, she said, to devote herself to the idea of restoration, even if she knew another two thousand years were to be needed for its realization.

It was not, however, in her nature to accept even an idea like Zionism without a penetrating analysis that saw the dangers involved. Speaking of the message to be found in the long line of Hebrew writers, she refers to their works as "instinct with Jewish consciousness which, kept in bounds, is self-respect. Kept in bounds, I repeat. If not restrained and disciplined by self-knowledge, self-respect degenerates into self-approval and eventually sinks into that most contemptible of qualities, national conceit or chauvinism."

Her activities in behalf of the Russians, deeply though they engaged her mind, constituted only part of the day's work. The regular school day of nine to three had to be followed by examination of papers and meticulous preparation of lessons. Yet her hours stretched to permit walks in the woods collecting botanical specimens, attendance at meetings of the Botany Club and the Woman's Literary Club, addresses to various local organizations, correspondence both personal and for the organizations of which she was never a merely passive member, articles for the English-Jewish press, volunteer work for the Jewish Publication Society, miscellaneous tasks of scholarship*—all added to the routine household tasks of gardening, marketing and sewing. For one who abhorred waste and could not tolerate idleness, it was fortunate that the active brain was matched by a vigorous physique.

* For example: The Jewish Home Prayer Book, 1888, based on a German manual of prayer prepared by Dr. Szold, bears in its introduction an acknowledgment of indebtedness to Miss Henrietta Szold for translation, elaboration, and valuable preparatory work.

4. *Jewish Publication Society*

"I accept the task life seems to have set me"

THE JEWISH Publication Society of America was organized in 1888, after failure by two earlier groups to carry out the functions of a publishing concern. Its founders believed that no people is great unless it possesses a great literature, that no people may hope to remain great unless it fosters its literary genius. The aim of the society was to produce a cultivated Jewry and to develop among the general public an atmosphere friendly to Jewish books.

When the venture was initiated American Jewry had neither the writers to produce English books on Jewish subjects, nor a reading public that called for the production of such literature. It was the function of the Jewish Publication Society to produce both writer and reader. It proved easier to produce the reader, for even after a membership list was on hand to ensure a modest beginning, an almost desperate search had to be made for authors.

Since the Society was an educational undertaking, operating on a non-profit basis, it depended on contributions and on the fees of its members. In order to keep expenses at a minimum, editorial work was shared by a body of scholars and experts who, in countless hours of reading and in conference with colleagues, contributed their services generously, each in his own specialty of religion, exegesis, law, sociology, history, education. The work of the Publication Committee has continued on that basis to the present.

Its first undertaking was *Outlines of Jewish History,* by Lady Magnus. The subject was chosen because the only history of the Jews then in print, by Henry Hart Milman, was considered incomplete, inaccurate and biased. The earliest publications were in large part English translations from German, French, Yiddish and Hebrew, of solid works of scholarship, written by men of established reputation. They included the writings of S. M. Dubnow and Heinrich Graetz in history; the philosophical-literary essays of Ahad Ha-Am (One of the People), pen-name of Asher Ginzberg; the short stories of Isaac Peretz; Professor Louis Ginzberg's studies in Jewish folklore; Moritz Lazarus on Jewish ethics; Nahum Slouschz on the rebirth of Hebrew literature. Other publications, written in English, were *Studies in Judaism,* by the great rabbinical scholar, Solomon Schechter, and Norman Bentwich's biographies of Philo and Josephus. From time to time novels, short stories and juvenilia lightened the list.

In 1892 the Society published Israel Zangwill's *Children of the Ghetto.* Its immediate popularity drew the attention of the general publisher to the possibility of interesting a wider public than that reached by the Jewish Publication Society. Macmillan published an edition for the general reader. Zangwill made warm acknowledgment to the Society, stating that without its stimulation he might never have written the book.

For many years Miss Szold worked as a volunteer member of the Society's Publication Committee. The report she presented on Graetz's *History of the Jews* revealed so many inaccuracies in the English translation that she was asked to accept the position of paid secretary to the Publication Committee. In 1893 the schoolteacher became a full-time editor. The break in occupation meant a break in family life for, in order to carry on her work efficiently, she settled in Philadelphia, home of the Jewish Publication Society, returning to Baltimore for weekends with her family. The year was saddened by personal loss. At the age of twenty-four, on the eve of marriage, Sadie Szold died.

As secretary to the Publication Committee, Henrietta's responsibilities were editing, proof-reading, translating and revising manuscripts, but more often than not the work of revision became a complete rewriting. Graetz's monumental work was one of those thorough-going revisions. To the original five volumes she added a sixth, the index, a painstaking piece of work of great value for reference. The translation of two of the four volumes of Professor Louis Ginzberg's *Legends of the Jews* was also hers, as was the English version of *Ethics of Judaism* by Morris Lazarus, a piece of work in which she took great satisfaction. To her other editorial tasks she added the annual compilation of *The American Jewish Year Book,* a statistical chronicle of the American Jewish community and its institutions.

Nothing remains of the official correspondence of this period. "It was the day of little things for me," she explained in a letter to Marvin Lowenthal. "I had no secretary to whom to dictate letters. I wrote them by hand on copying paper. The time came when the contracted office couldn't afford to give space to the voluminous correspondence with authors who allowed no minute change in style or even punctuation without discussion and argumentation. The manager decreed destruction by fire. So one day when I arrived at the office, I stood before a mountainous pile which presently was consigned to the fire with Hitlerian pitilessness."

A year after the death of her father in 1902, Henrietta settled herself and her mother in their first New York home, an apartment on West 123rd Street, opposite the early home of the Jewish Theological Seminary. There she attended lectures, the better to prepare herself for the task of editing her father's manuscripts.

By 1916, when her secretaryship ended, close to one hundred volumes had been issued under the imprint of the Jewish Publication Society. Fifty-four authors had been introduced to the Jewish reading public of America, and stimulus had been given to the production, on American soil, of literature dealing with subjects of Jewish interest.

Application to editing and translating did not preclude intensive work at voluntary tasks. The Federation of American Zionists, later the Zionist Organization of America, counted Henrietta among its most active and dependable workers. One time-consuming job after another was assigned to her. She wondered whether the demands were legitimate or whether she considered them legitimate because she hadn't the stamina to turn them down. In vain she protested: "Because I must hold myself ready to meet a thousand claims from the outside, I have neglected my own little garden. I am not allowed to mature what is in me, because I must do all the time—morning, noon, and night—what others impose upon me. Some years ago I resigned myself to my fate; I no longer kick against the traces. I accept the task life seems to have set me."

In turn Miss Szold was member of the Executive Committee of the Federation of American Zionists, its honorary vice-president, and its honorary secretary. The Zionist dictionary, she said, defined honor as work. Each post brought its duties and responsibilities. The hours after five which were devoted to those duties constituted a second day's work in every twenty-four hours. Among the most exacting of the tasks was that of bringing order into the financial records which had, by some one's carelessness, become a mess of disordered, unrelated and dust-laden figures.

For many years Miss Szold pleaded for a library which should contain every publication related to Palestine and the development of Zionist activities. In the present Zionist Archives of America, established in the late 1930's, the only copies to be found of many early Zionist publications are those with her name inscribed on their title pages. The fact throws a sidelight on her sense of historical continuity and on her understanding of the value of preserving the documents as part of the records of her people.

More rewarding was the association with visitors from Palestine who sought her advice and assistance. Among these was Aaron Aaronsohn, the agronomist whose search for wild wheat ended in success on the slopes of Mount Hermon. The world of science hailed the discovery with enthusiasm, for it made possible the strengthening of the known varieties of wheat which, in centuries of cultivation, had lost their powers of resistance to disease. Through Miss Szold's agency, non-Zionist Jews—Louis Marshall, Julius Rosenwald, Professor Morris Loeb—gave generously to further the research activities of Aaronsohn's Agricultural Experiment Station at Athlit.

Short visits with her sisters—with Rachel Jastrow in Madison or on Mount Desert, with Bertha in Baltimore—punctuated the routine of work without fully interrupting it, for the ever-present galleys of the proofreader trailed along with her. In Baltimore she found additional delight in the company and antics of the five lively nieces and nephews who had taken possession of Bertha's household.

The year 1915 wrote finis to the arduous life of an editor. Thanks to the far-sightedness of Judge Julian W. Mack and others, Miss Szold was henceforth relieved of the necessity of earning her living. Their discernment enabled her to make of herself a gift to the Jewish people, and the rest of her days were devoted entirely to its service. "I want you to know," she wrote to Judge Mack in 1942, "that what your friendship prompted you to do for me I recognize to have been the great opportunity that has made my latter years active and—may I add in all modesty?—productive."

Miss Szold now intensified her Zionist activities, making her main task that of welding the three-year-old Hadassah into a formidably strong organization (See Chapter 5). Encouraged by the Balfour Declaration, the Zionist Organization of America was expanding its work. In 1918 an Education Department was established; for its organization and activities Henrietta Szold became responsible. With the able assistance of Emanuel Neumann (recently president of the Zionist Organization of America), she coordinated the activities of several groups—Young Judaea, Histadruth Ivrith (a Hebrew culture society), the Intercollegiate Zionists—and their respective publications. For two years the Department made strides, producing and circulating informative material, establishing a library of books, pamphlets, and slides, and running a mail order book business—all of which resulted in a general stimulation of interest and activity.

Soon after Miss Szold's departure for Palestine early in 1920, dwindling financial income caused the Zionist Organization to disband the Education Department. To Henrietta Szold it was an inexcusable step, indicating a short-sighted policy. "Please believe me," she wrote from Palestine, "when I say that the passing of the Education Department does not affect me because I put so much effort into its upbuilding. What I fear is the passing of the spirit that made Zionism a real force."

Work absorbed her to such an extent that there was no time to form friendships with those who stood outside her circles of work. It was through her varied undertakings that she made most of her personal contacts. Some assumed that the desire and the need for friendship were non-existent. Nothing could be wider of the mark. Never did Henrietta become too old to form new associations and loyal friendships with those who found their way to her side.

Her New York apartment, across the street from the Jewish Theological Seminary, was a Mecca for students and professors. Newcomers from Europe—Professors Friedlaender, Marx and Ginzberg—came to her regularly for assistance with the English form of their lectures. Dr. Solomon Schechter, brilliant head of the Seminary, loved to walk and talk with his "Minerva." The writing he begged her to do she never had time for. Professor and Mrs. Marx looked forward to her weekly evening visits to their home with her mother, almost the only social relaxation she allowed herself. She joined her hostess in duets at the piano, her musicianship allowing easy and competent playing of the Beethoven symphonies. She explained to Mrs. Marx, unfamiliar with the English language, the fascinating mysteries of Robert Browning.

At this time she first met and talked with Judah Magnes: "It was in 1904. My mother had gone to Baltimore on a visit. On Saturday afternoon I was alone in the house when the bell rang. I went to the door. A gentleman stood there, a young man looking full of youth. He said,

'My name is Magnes, and I have been thinking we ought to know each other, so I came.' "

Dearest of all her friends was Alice Seligsberg, New York social worker, to whom Henrietta once wrote: "Life has not been mean to me since you are my friend." The friendship was solace when her mother's death in 1916 left her alone with her memories of rosy cheeks and blue eyes, alert activities and equally alert interests, busy hands and undaunted courage—the picture of a beautifully rounded life, useful and happy in spite of its great trials. In the turmoil of her arrival in Palestine in 1920, it was the sight of Alice at the station that brought serenity because Alice represented home.

Henrietta in Jerusalem and Alice in New York carried on an active correspondence on matters political, social and personal, particularly those bearing on developments in Palestine. Actually the relationship was not a dual, but a triangular one, Mrs. Edward Jacobs, president of Hadassah for many years, forming the third point of the triangle. It was Rose Jacobs whose presence in Palestine Miss Szold begged for when crucial decisions were in the making. To these two she poured out her doubts, her trials, her plans, and the innermost hopes of her heart. It was on them she leaned for sound and disinterested judgment. There was not always agreement on method or on objective, but confidence in one another's integrity characterized their relations to the end. The loss of Alice in the summer of 1940 left Henrietta bereaved and mourning. "Superficial observers," she wrote then, "might have thought that she came under my influence. The reverse was the case . . . No meeting with her left me as I had been before. There was always some addition to my spiritual store."

5. *Hadassah, the Women's Zionist Organization*

"The healing of my people"

THE FIRST fifty years of Henrietta Szold's life might be considered a preamble. Not that she was not doing important work, and doing it to perfection. But it was work of a type others could do and were doing. In her fifties her real originality was called into play. From that time forward her genius found its full expression.

The nucleus of Hadassah—at this writing it numbers 300,000 members—was a group of fifteen women. Called the Hadassah Study Circle, it had been devoting itself over a period of years to the study and discussion of Judaism and Zionism. Hess, Pinsker, Ahad Ha-Am, Herzl—the founding fathers—were familiar to the members as more than names. The meetings were entirely informal, conducted without benefit of chairman. After Miss Szold's introduction to the Study Circle, the acknowledgment was tacit that where Miss Szold sat, there was the head of the table.

Her association with the group began in 1907 after the receipt of a letter from Dr. Judah L. Magnes, then incumbent of the pulpit at Temple Emanuel, New York. Dr. Magnes was one of the few Reform Rabbis who had at that time embraced Zionism. His letter invited Miss Szold to become an honorary member of the Hadassah Circle. That at least was the tenor of the invitation, though the suspicion may be entertained that some unexpressed purpose lurked in the writer's mind. Miss Szold accepted the invitation on the characteristic condition that she be accepted as an active member of the group: "If I go into that, I have to go into it myself and do something about it."

In 1909 Miss Szold and her mother visited Palestine. She had toured Scotland, England, France, Austro-Hungary, Turkey, Egypt, Syria. She had been interested in the past of each country because otherwise she could not understand the present. In Palestine it was past, present, and future that concerned her. She traveled about the country by wagon, visiting fourteen colonies and the cities of Tiberias, Haifa and Jaffa. In Jerusalem she spent twelve days, some of them in company with Professor and Mrs. Richard Gottheil. The misery and disease in the cities made her heartsick, as did the evidence she saw of mismanagement and of chaos in education. But the land itself evoked unqualified enthusiasm as she spoke of the sky by day and by night, the hillsides, the valleys, the mountain tops, the incredible fertility and the abrupt contrasts. "How can travellers return with any but one opinion upon its desirability? I learned to love its grayness, its stones, its terraces, its varied richnesses. It is the only possible refuge for our people. If we fail, I see no hope for our fragments." On the eve of the rains, she described the heat, the heavy silence and insupportable oppression of the evening atmosphere:

> No color anywhere except the orange in the sky and in the notes of the cornet, but in the thick black hedge that divided the garden from the fields stretch-

ing away to the orange groves against the horizon, something gleamed—a single, still, pure, white myrtle blossom. Hadassah! Was it a belated blossom? Was it a precocious herald of spring? If only the tired workmen inside would come and look at it! Their unexplainable weariness and hopelessness would drop away from them. It would make Reb Mendel sing a merry Hassidic song, and they all would be happy again . . .

"Comrades, brothers, the rain is coming! The early rain is here at last!" It was Reb Jehudah singing the glad immemorial song of the Palestinian farmer.

And the rain splashed down in great, long drops. The pall of darkness was lifted from tree and house and earth. The orange glow was dispelled. The cornet broke off in the middle of a discordant orange note. Happy human voices mingled with the rush of the rain. The young laborers embraced each other. Jubilating they ran into the garden, and on their upturned, tired faces the rain came down as upon mown grass. The showers that watered the earth descended upon them and revived their souls. Through the gray masses of down-pouring water, the eye caught glimpses of the blues and pinks and purples of the Palestinian air.

Now it was certain—the hadassah blossom was the harbinger of spring.

The impressions received left their mark. The full result of Henrietta Szold's experiences was not to be bound within words: the seeds there implanted in her mind were to come to fruition in deeds. At the time she could not know that. What she did know was that all her powers had been called forth and kept alert during the four weeks of her stay in Palestine. If only she were twenty years younger, she felt, her field of work would lie here. Thus in 1909. It was not until February, 1920, that she again set sail for Palestine, remaining there, except for more or less brief periods, until her death in February, 1945, aged eighty-four, active until the last few months of her life.

"It's my eyes, not my brain," she once wrote. "So long as I can keep my eyes open, I must work for amelioration." And her eyes had looked upon the children of Palestine, their scrawny legs, their sick, fly-ridden eyes. They had seen also the healthy eyes of the pupils at the Jewish Girls' School in Jaffa. Mystified, she turned to the principal, Dr. Touroff, for an explanation. "There is no mystery here, dear lady. It is only that we have physicians and a nurse who visit us regularly and keep the children's eyes clean and healthy."

On her return to America, Miss Szold presented her ideas to the Hadassah Study Circle. It brought a new orientation to the group—organization on a national scale, with the specific aims of practical work in Palestine, education in America. Two years of preparatory discussion and planning laid the groundwork. Then the call for organization went out:

> The undersigned, in consultation with other women Zionists in North America, have reached the conclusion that the time is ripe for a large organization of women Zionists, and they desire to invite you to attend a meeting for the purpose of discussing the feasibility of forming an organization which shall have for its purpose the promotion of Jewish institutions and enterprises in Palestine, and the fostering of Jewish ideals.
>
> The meeting will be held February 24th, at eight

P.M., in the Vestry Rooms of Temple Emanu-El, Fifth Avenue and Forty-third Street.

Sophia Berger
Gertrude Goldsmith
Emma Gottheil (Mrs. Richard)
Lotta Levensohn
Rosalie S. Phillips (Mrs. N. Taylor)
Mathilde Schechter (Mrs. S.)
Henrietta Szold

New York, February 14, 1912

At Purim, the Feast of Esther, 1912, fifteen women, augmented by another twenty-three, constituted themselves the Hadassah Chapter of a projected national body to be known as Daughters of Zion. Hadassah, Queen Esther's Hebrew name (derived from *hadas,* Hebrew for myrtle), was adopted both as continuing the name of the original group and as appropriate to Purim, the birthday of the infant organization. Each Chapter, as it was organized, would call itself by the name of some Jewish heroine. For the time being the funds collected would be used to establish a system of district visiting nursing in the towns and colonies, the first nurse to be equipped for Jerusalem and to be known as the New York Nurse. In America study circles were to be established for women, and Jewish educational work undertaken among children.

The original body of officers was:

President, Henrietta Szold; Vice Presidents, Mrs. R. Gottheil, Mrs. Lewin-Epstein, Mrs. N. Taylor Phillips; Recording Secretary, Miss Rachel Natelson; Corresponding Secretary, Miss Rose Herzog; Treasurer, Miss Nettie Illoway; Board of Directors, Mrs. S. Schechter, Dr. Anna Willner, Mrs. M. M. Kaplan, Mrs. S. P. Abelow, Mrs. J. L. Magnes, Mrs. C. Ruskay, Miss Alice Seligsberg, Miss Sarah

Kussy, Miss Rebecca Aronson, Miss Sophia Berger, Miss Gertrude Goldsmith, Miss Rose Jaine, Miss Lotta Levensohn.

Need was felt for a motto for the new-born baby. For this Miss Szold turned to Professor Israel Friedlaender of the Jewish Theological Seminary. His suggestion of a phrase from Jeremiah was accepted: "Behold the voice of the cry of my people from a land that is very far off . . . Is there no balm in Gilead? Is there no physician there? Why then is not the healing of my people accomplished?" (Jeremiah, 8:19, 22) The phrase of despair became the emblem of a forceful purpose.

In the nurture of the infant body Miss Szold's ideas on organization and education had full play and the infant grew steadily through lusty childhood to full maturity. The early history of Zionism in the United States had seen many women's groups forming and reforming, going through periods of activity only to end in disintegration. Members married and, absorbed by household duties, forgot their Zionist obligations. The new organization was to develop in them a sense of responsibility toward their people and their people's land, and to provide a broad, general platform on which all shades of social and political opinion could meet.

The announced purpose of the organization brought down on the heads of Miss Szold and her associates bitter and jeering criticism. They were denounced by enraged Zionists both for organizing a separate women's body and for laying out a program of mere charity. Miss Szold took up the challenge. "I am not going to deal with generalities," she said, "I know what the pitfalls of generalities are." She explained that the barriers separating Jewish women and Jewish women had to be broken down—as that, for instance, between the American-born and the foreign-born; she declared that women would respond to the appeal of a definite, practical objective: "Not charity. I deny it. We go to Palestine equipped, as American Jewish women particularly are, with philanthropic and social work, with the purpose of bringing to Palestine the results of American healing art . . . If we can do that service to Palestine . . . if we can bring order to that land of chaos, that charge cannot be brought against us, that we are a charitable society."

Not once, but many times, Miss Szold was forced to face the charge that, in Hadassah, Zionism was degenerating into charity. She was prepared to accept the charge if charity were interpreted in its largest sense as love. The attacks continued; she quoted Herzl's dictum: "Philanthropy to a whole people is politics." In America she had at least the comfort of a sturdy regiment of women at her back, whose support and understanding she could count upon. In Palestine, where in one field after another she sought to bring clarity and order into chaos, the struggle was long and bitter. Years of effort that might have gone into productive activity had to be spent in fighting opposition forces which, blinded by their slogans, failed to grasp the essential rightness of her thinking.

By the end of Hadassah's first year, 157 regular members and 37 associate members, had been enrolled; $542 had been collected in dues.

By June, 1914, the Daughters of Zion held its first national convention at Rochester, New York. Representatives had come together from seven Chapters out of a total of eight. They were:

Kadimah, of Baltimore
Clara de Hirsch, of Chicago
Shoshannah, of Cleveland

Ruth, of Newark
Hadassah, of New York
Rebecca Gratz, of Philadelphia
Lady Zionists, of St. Paul

The Boston Chapter, Deborah, was not represented.

Swayed largely by the arguments of Dr. Judah L. Magnes, the delegates voted to drop the name "Daughters of Zion" in favor of the more euphonious and more richly connotative one of "Hadassah." The latter name, placed over the door of the settlement-clinic to which the patients resorted, had already established itself in Palestine.

Miss Szold's concern with cultural values led to emphasis on the development of leaders in America through intensive study. The members of those early years who attended study groups and parlor meetings have not forgotten how generously Miss Szold gave of herself, day after day and week after week, never failing to appear punctually, no matter how tardy others were, even in weather so forbidding that she would find only two or three present out of the more or less regular group of seven or eight auditors. She opened up the pages of the Jewish past to those whose curriculum of study might have covered German, French, Latin, Greek, history ancient and modern, but not by the remotest chance Jewish history or the Hebrew language. "Know thyself" might have been taken as the motto for her motivation.

There was careful design and forethought in her program for the general membership of the organization, and for those whose preoccupation with home and children made attendance at study groups impossible. Every activity of the budding organization was forced to yield its quota of Jewish and Zionist education. A National Fund box? No placing of a box, no collection from a box without conversation explaining the why and the wherefore, without discussion of some recent event in Palestine or Diaspora. A prospective member? No membership without understanding and acceptance of the Basle Platform—a publicly recognized, legally secured home in Palestine for the Jewish people. No acceptance of tempting membership dues to Hadassah as to a philanthropic body, but only as identification of self with the wider implications of membership—rehabilitation of a people. On these terms only could membership be solicited and dues accepted—on no other terms, since quality was the desideratum, not quantity for the sake of quantity.

Contributions were welcomed from those not adhering to the political program of the organization, but they were never used for any other purpose than welfare work; no part of them was ever assigned to defray the expenses of what was fundamentally a political organization. "Our associate members," wrote Gertrude Goldsmith (later Mrs. Bernard Rosenblatt), "are likely to plead with us to gain in numbers and wealth, rather than in small accessions of Zionist converts who are so often poor in worldly goods. Since to know a danger is the first step in guarding against it, we hope you will realize this danger, and will see that your Chapter remains Zionist to the core." The situation sometimes led to difficulties, as in the case of the prospective group which requested that a speaker be sent, but specified that that speaker must not use the word "Zionism."

Other means also were used to give the membership a sense of close connection with Palestine. Letters, giving word pictures of conditions, accompanied the reports of the two nurses established in Jerusalem. Published in the *Hadassah Bulletin,* forerunner of the present *Newsletter,* these letters gave the American women a sense of intimacy, almost of proprietorship, in Palestine, thereby helping to foster and further Hadassah's concrete purpose.

Junior Hadassah came into being during Miss Szold's absence in Palestine. An appeal to her to suggest a motto brought it flashing across the oceans: *Em Banim Smecha* (A Joyful Mother of Children). Through her foresight the Juniors received the opportunity to exercise autonomy from the outset of their existence. Their demand for self-direction met with opposition from their elders. Miss Szold arose and acclaimed the youthful body. "Let the Juniors be our guides," she exhorted the skeptical seniors. Her respect inspired the young people with confidence; it drew out and brought to the fore qualities of which the Juniors themselves were hardly aware.

She was not of those who railed at the younger generation for following other roads than hers and adopting other patterns: "The successive generations have and must demand qualities and methods other than those of the former generation. Life exacts work from them under other conditions."

Whether she was in the States or beyond the two oceans, the Juniors continued to turn to her. At one point, much troubled as to the roads that lay before them and unable to come to a decision, they appealed to her for direction. Replying, she told them of her father. When she was a little bit of a thing, she wrote them, she would come to her father with her childish problems and ask him what to do. "I cannot tell you what to do," he had said to her then. "I can only analyze the situation. You must decide for yourself." Now she turned the same words on the Juniors. "You have taken up some of the burdens of life and therefore no one can direct you. You must be the captains of your own selves . . . I can only tell you what the situation is in Palestine, and then each one of you will have to work things out for yourself."

To watch Miss Szold presiding at a meeting of her Central Committee was an intellectual treat. As each problem, each new situation, came up for examination, members of the Committee offered their varying views. There was never any attempt on the part of the Chairman to dictate, or even to influence decisions. She was their agent, her function being to carry out the decisions determined upon by them. "The problem is before you. What do you want me to do about it?" But when, having completed their own examination of the problem, they turned to her with, "But, Miss Szold, what do you think about it?" the probing mind revealed facets that had occurred to no one else and plumbed depths unfathomed by the others.

The Central Committee of Hadassah was a homogeneous and disciplined group, imbued with sincerity of purpose, its sole aim the good of the organization for which all labored. Differences of opinion there necessarily were, but never were those differences permitted to interrupt, much less disrupt, the smooth functioning of the group. Varying points of view, given their due weight in discussion, were submerged in majority decisions, and harmony marked the action taken by the Committee. In such an atmosphere there was no room and no reason for personal rivalries and ambitions; no struggle for office, no striving for publicity or prestige. The aim of each was to advance the work, "certain that almost all, if not all, will agree that the work alone and not the workers should be in evidence." To each her task in consonance with her individual gifts and the contribution those gifts could bring; to all the satisfaction of comradeship in a vital undertaking and joy in accomplishment.

Appraising the work of the organization on its twenty-fifth anniversary, Miss Szold said: "The most significant result was achieved by Hadassah in the course of its first quarter of a century; for the American result bears within itself an eternal promise, the promise of ever-renewing action . . . When Hadassah's crowning medical undertaking began to pass from vision to reality on Scopus, the sisterhood in America, with pristine enthusiasm and swift vigor . . . leapt to the accomplishment of a new purpose, the release of youth from political and spiritual bondage. Purpose after purpose may disappear through fulfillment; the force that originated and perfected each one will persist and produce new values in conformity with the needs and demands of new times."

No greater tribute can be paid to the architect than has been given by the years. The structure she laid with sure hand has withstood time and its shocks, has gone from strength to strength, the instrument of many proud achievements. Her own proud statement—or may we call it boast?—came in answer to a proposal from the women in Palestine to "appeal" to Hadassah for funds to meet certain emergency needs. "No," she said, "to Hadassah we send no 'appeal'. To Hadassah we send only information . . . To Hadassah we tell only what the need is."

6. *Hadassah Medical Organization*

"Here he is painting the whole background"

THE REASON that the Jews come to Palestine, the reason that you Jewish youth love to be here is that here the Jewish creative ability is allowed free play. In other lands the Jew can perhaps put a few strokes into the background of the picture, but here he is painting the whole background." The words were spoken in conversation with Ruth Light (Mrs. Boris Kazman), a young artist from New York, who had succeeded in getting Miss Szold to sit for her.

As we have seen, Henrietta Szold's first visit to Palestine determined the future course of her life and her share in painting the background. "This is your work, Henrietta; this is what your Hadassah should be doing," her mother had said, pointing to the children's eyes and their scrawny legs.

In 1912, when Miss Szold's organization plans began to function, there was in existence in Jerusalem a Jewish Health Bureau established by the New York philanthropist, Nathan Straus. Conducted by Drs. Bruenn and Goldberg, its principal functions were to combat malaria and trachoma. There was a Pasteur Institute, under the direction of Dr. Beham, sponsored by a group of German Jewish physicians in Palestine. There were four Jewish hospitals, two Old Folks' Homes, an Institute for the Blind, and the Lemaan Zion Eye Clinic presided over by Dr. Ticho.

In the larger cities, five to ten persons lived in one or two rooms, without water, light, sufficient air, frequently without food. Under such conditions and under the care of midwives who knew nothing of sepsis and antisepsis, seventy-five percent of the Jewish women bore their children —those who could not or would not resort to the missionary hospitals. Amulets and incantations were remedies in general use. Ignorance plus unsanitary surroundings plus low resistance due to poverty resulted in an appalling mortality. Not one of the Jewish hospitals had a maternity ward. The existing Christian hospitals were missionary in character. They made use of the physical needs and ills of the Jews in order to wean them from their ancestral faith. No medication without a Christian sermon; no bed without the services of a preacher of Christianity. Cases were reported of the baptism, without the parents' knowledge, of new-born children.

Hadassah's immediate task, to be begun as soon as the necessary funds were in hand, was to be the establishment of a system of district nursing service, modeled upon that of the Henry Street Settlement in New York. The service was to have social and educational as well as medical aspects, and these would help in regenerating people and land. The American organization looked forward to having a peace regiment of Jewish district nurses ministering to the towns and villages of Palestine. It might even be possible, eventually, to establish a training school for nurses, perhaps even a maternity hospital and a children's hospital. This was a daring vision that belonged not to any immediate reality but to a distant and nebulous future.

For the present the membership was small and the collections were meager. But help was coming. Nathan Straus of blessed memory, merchant prince and prince of men, had heard of the Hadassah program. Besides his Health Bureau he was maintaining a soup kitchen for the poor of Jerusalem. "Once, long ago," he explained to Miss Szold, "I suffered the pangs of hunger. I was starving. I had no money for a single meal for a few days. I have never forgotten the sensation. In so far as lies within my power, no man that crosses my path shall go hungry."

Nathan Straus and his wife Lina invited Miss Szold to visit them, and inquired solicitously about her plans. She gave them the information they wanted, but did not ask for help. The next day the Strauses returned her visit, climbing the three flights of stairs to her apartment. On the first occasion Mr. Straus had asked her, "Why don't you start work?" On this visit to her they reverted to the same query, repeating it more than once during the conversation. Miss Szold's answer was the only one possible—$273 in the treasury. "Begin," urged Mrs. Straus, winking behind her husband's back. "Begin, have faith, and the rest will follow of itself." But beginning an enterprise without assured prospect of its continuation was not Henrietta Szold's method. Finally the old man could contain himself no longer, and revealed the purpose which had brought him. He offered to provide fare for the passage of two nurses, payment of part of the first year's salary and furnishings for the settlement house, on condition that the nurses be chosen at once and equipped for immediate sailing.

Within three weeks twenty-one applicants were interviewed; the election fell on Rose Kaplan and Rachel

Landy, and on January 18, 1913, they sailed in company with Lina and Nathan Straus and Miss Eva Leon,* who had been active in welfare work for Palestine. On March 23 the settlement was in operation. By the end of the first year the settlement-clinic which was the nurses' home was the center of bustling activity. A part-time physician was ministering gratis to the poor; daily trachoma treatments were being given to schoolchildren in twenty-one schools; an assisting oculist was established at the Lemaan Zion Eye Clinic; six midwives were delivering mothers under expert supervision; extra diet and clothing were being distributed to destitute patients; anemia treatments were being given to clinic patients who were also receiving information and friendly advice; two clubs for "Little Mothers" had been established.

Soon after the outbreak of World War I, both nurses were forced to return to the United States, Rose Kaplan for an immediate surgical operation, and Miss Landy because of serious illness in her family. Miss Kaplan, knowing herself doomed, returned later to resume work among the Palestinian refugees† in Alexandria, dying there on August 3, 1919. But in Jerusalem the work was continuing. It had been well systematized by the nurses and was being carried on under the able supervision of Dr. Helena Kaghan.

It was a pauper country across which the opposing hosts were fighting. Sights commonplace to survivors of the recent holocaust were, earlier in the century, novel and horrifying. "Never in my life," wrote Miss Landy before her return, "will I forget these last few weeks . . . You should see the people in the streets. They are perfect

* Sister-in-law of Professor Richard Gottheil, first president of the Federation of American Zionists.

† All residents of Palestine, who were not subjects of Turkey, had been expelled from the country.

studies in pain, misery and starvation. I never saw such faces. You can imagine how it feels to approach them, and they are ashamed to approach you . . . The Straus Soup Kitchen is open. What a blessing it is!"

At war's outbreak all physicians of alien citizenship, which meant by far the larger number of Jewish medical men resident in Palestine, had been deported. Of those remaining most had been impressed into army service. Ravaged by diseases—cholera, typhus, malaria—the few who remained were hard put to it to minister to the needs of a hungry and ailing population. The supply of drugs was exhausted. Hospitals were shut down because the buildings had been requisitioned by the military.

Jerusalem, with a pre-war Jewish population of 50,000, was served by three physicians. A clinic opened by Dr. Kaghan had a small waiting room, a smaller consultation room. Patients blocked the streets outside it. Children were left in the streets by mothers who, no able-bodied men being available, had been pressed into service for the building of the Jerusalem-Bethlehem road. The clinic became a twelve-bed hospital. Later a day-nursery was opened, with straw mats for equipment and other supplies begged here and there. While their filthy clothing was being washed, the children waited, wrapped in sheets. At night they were taken home, kicking and screaming their protest. The Red Cross, arriving with the victorious British armies, eased the situation somewhat with supplies of linens, blankets, and food.

Such was the situation in Palestine when Hadassah in America held its third annual convention in July, 1916, and listened to a sensational announcement by its Central Committee. The announcement concerned a communication received one month earlier. Sent by the World Zionist Organization to its American arm, the Provisional Executive Committee for Zionist Affairs, the communication stressed the extreme need of Palestine for a body of physcians and nurses. Such a medical force, when organized, would be known as the American Zionist Medical Unit. The Committee turned to Hadassah. By that time Hadassah had acquired a membership of 1937 women and was looking hopefully toward a round figure of 2000. The receipts for the convention year just completed totaled $2880.46.

The delegates listened appalled. Could this infant body, just past its fourth birthday, undertake the responsibility? Did they dare shoulder the task of raising the huge sum of $25,000—the bare minimum necessary for equipping, transporting and maintaining for one year a medical force of ten physicians and two nurses?

By fall the $25,000 minimum had risen to $30,000, and the women were told, in explanation, that their medical undertaking should be conducted generously, in accordance with every demand of up-to-date science. It should be worthy of the land which they looked upon as the hope of their nation; it should be in keeping with the merits and the sufferings of the pioneers, who were working hard to make the land a fit home for themselves, their children, and the whole Jewish people. By this time staff needs were estimated at ten physicians and five nurses.

Funds were to be raised by self-taxation. If every one of the 2000 women contributed $15, the required amount would be raised. It was a great deal to ask, said Miss Szold; some sacrifices might be necessary, such as saving on carfares and putting the nickels thus saved into the medical fund.

For selecting personnel and securing equipment there was an advisory board, of which the chairman was Dr. Harry Friedenwald, ophthalmologist, past president of the Zionist Organization, life-long friend of Henrietta Szold. His co-workers were Dr. Isaac A. Abt, Chicago; Drs. Isaac Adler and Emanuel Libman of New York; Dr. Milton J. Rosenau, of the Harvard Medical School; and Miss Lillian D. Wald, of the Nurses' Settlement, New York. In the Zionist offices, Henrietta Szold, Jacob de Haas, Secretary of the Provisional Committee, and Adolph Hubbard devoted themselves to the preparations—interviewing applicants, handling passport, visa and export license technicalities, locating and purchasing supplies—an unenviable task at a time when the United States was in the grip of a war economy.

Negotiations with the warring countries, to permit the passage of the Medical Unit through blockaded waters, dragged on for months. They were not concluded until some months after Allenby's entry into Jerusalem in December, 1917. Meanwhile rising prices and an expanding program had raised the original estimate of $25,000 to $75,000, then to $100,000.

A year rolled by, and again Hadassah was sitting in convention, listening to its leader's report: "The future is full of the gravest responsibilities. We are promised a place in the sun—not to ravage and dominate, but to serve our people, ourselves, the world. Standing in the sun we shall be seen clearly as never before. Our abilities will be on trial before a world full of nations, who will judge us in the light of a glorious past of ideal service to mankind. For Israel election has never meant anything but obligation. Clearly, rehabilitating a nation is not a pastime. It is a task, a heavy task, a holy task."

By April, 1918, the project had grown from one requiring a half ton of supplies to one requiring four hundred tons, sufficient to equip and supply a fifty-bed hospital including surgical instruments, drugs, medicines, bandages, dental outfits, six automobiles, two ambulances, two trucks, large quantities of food and one hundred large cases of clothing. The personnel now numbered forty-five—twenty physicians, twenty nurses, and five administrators. The cost of maintaining the Unit for one year was estimated, moderately, at $50,000. The sum was to be provided jointly by the American Jewish Joint Distribution Committee, the Zionist Organization of America, the Palestine Restoration Fund, and Hadassah. In Chicago, in Kansas City, in Boston, in communities all across the country, small bands of women set themselves devotedly to the task of scraping together nickels, dimes and dollars. The coins were paving a wide road and a long one, and Hadassah and its founder were painting in their share of the background in bold and significant strokes.

On June 12, 1918, at 4 A.M., the American Zionist Medical Unit set sail. It traveled on the *Megantic,* in convoy, with three submarine zones to be crossed before it could reach its destination. Without a medical director, since the physician appointed had abandoned his post a few weeks before the sailing, the Unit sailed in charge of two lay administrators—Alice Seligsberg and Adolph Hubbard. Months later Dr. Isaac M. Rubinow, statistician and authority on social insurance, arrived in Palestine to direct the activities of the Unit.

During the long period of preparation and waiting, the personnel had taken part in conferences, listened to lectures on Palestine, attended classes in Hebrew and studied with specialists on tropical diseases, public health, district nursing and other professional procedures. On board they continued their training. By day, drills, lectures, prayers. By night, darkness and apprehension. One night a tremor passed through the convoy; the next morning a ship was missing.

Landing in Liverpool, they found their further journey from London blocked by the niceties or vagaries of wartime diplomacy. (Did the fact that Alice Seligsberg was of German parentage, and that both she and Henrietta Szold were members of a women's peace organization have something to do with these vargaries? In 1920 that membership accounted for Miss Szold's enforced sojourn of six weeks in Italy, awaiting the arrival of a British visa permitting her to enter Palestine. Two later voyages to Palestine were held up for the same reason, awaiting special action by British officialdom.) Five weeks' delay in London was followed by ten days encamped at Taranto, because of submarine activity in the Mediterranean. Finally, on August 11, the Unit reached Alexandria, standing at life-boat stations and wearing their life belts. Troops of camels—25,000 of them—were seen carrying water up through the desert. It was the prelude, though of that they had no foreknowledge, of the final routing of the Turks at Megiddo. At Alexandria, Dr. Chaim Weizmann, head of the World Zionist Organization, was on hand to greet them. So were the sights and sounds—and characteristic smells—of the Orient.

An emergency had called the Unit into being. A dread development met them—cholera in Tiberias, with 75% of the population infected. Traveling on horseback all day and all night, the relief force of physicians and nurses reached the city at dawn, to be received at its gates by weeping and praying throngs.

One of the nurses, Anna Kaplan,* was delayed in London by illness. She pictured conditions in Tel Aviv as she found them a few months later. The town was all but open desert. It consisted of one short street, a few

* Director of Nursing Service in Hadassah Medical Organization and Principal of School of Nursing, 1920-1927.

scattered houses and the Herzl Academy. In all directions sand dunes extended, and the refuse and rubbish left by the occupying armies—Turkish, German, Italian, French. Camels and Bedouins squatted everywhere. The hospital, a two-story private house, had been whitewashed by the nurses. Every bed was occupied; the sick had been picked up on the beaches, helpless from heat, fever, and thirst. Mosquito netting had been placed over the beds. A combination supply closet-desk was a shipping case covered by a bed sheet; a smaller case was a chair. Kerosene lamps supplied the lighting. The service suffered from a serious water shortage and bad plumbing.

In the out-patient department camels, donkeys, and goats shared the waiting space with patients. Everywhere filth and flies—endless flies—in nostrils, ears and mouths. One patient, intent on private remedies, was busy rubbing manure into his skin infection.

In Jerusalem, the Rothschild Hospital, a beautiful two-story building of rose-colored granite, had one lavatory, no bathrooms, no running water, no lighting or heating system, poor plumbing.

To reach the Safed Hospital meant a three-day trip by train, wagon and donkey. One Primus stove supplied all the needs of the hospital. When an operation was in progress and the Primus was needed in the operating room, the patients went without cooked food. There was not a Primus in the country to be had for love or money. Neither could one purchase needles, thread, materials, clothing, shoes, utensils, furniture or cow's milk or many other vital materials. Months passed before orders for such items could be filled.

Such were the conditions in towns and cities. In Tel Hai, a northern settlement newly established close to the Syrian border, the dining table was constructed of two barrels at either end of the shed, with boards laid across. After the destruction of the roof in an Arab attack, the room was knee-deep in water. A traveler who was given the last available room found himself sharing it with a horse from which he was separated by a burlap curtain.

Under such general living conditions a high sickness rate was not surprising. Dr. Rubinow's report attributed the high incidence of sickness to poor and insufficient food, exposure to changes of weather without proper clothing, unhygienic buildings, tent-living, mosquitoes and, above all, ignorance. He found the climate salubrious and the country not at all the pest-hole it had been represented by enemies of the National Home.

Within a few years the work of the organization—now known officially as the Hadassah Medical Organization—had permeated every corner of Jewish life in Palestine. It was impossible to walk into any city or agricultural settlement without noting the all-pervading presence of Hadassah—the infant welfare station, the malaria control unit, the playgrounds, school hygiene, school luncheons, home visiting, distribution of pasteurized milk—all within five years of the establishment of the original Unit.

Hospitals and infant welfare stations imply nursing service. Except for a school at Beirut the Middle East had no institutions for professional training in nursing. The establishment of a school was one of the immediate tasks of the Unit. In spite of the scant respect in which the nursing profession was held, and in defiance of family opposition, young women pleaded and clamored for admittance to the school. Only those were accepted who could meet the standards set for health and previous education.

Although Hebrew was necessarily the language of instruction, the teaching had to proceed without a single Hebrew text. Not a typewriter was available equipped with

Hebrew characters; lectures were copied by scribes and copies given to each student. There were no regular classrooms. The Nurses Home was at some distance from the hospital, and in the rainy season, no transportation being available, the nurses plodded up and down the unpaved hill through a thick soup of mud.

The graduation of the first class took place on November 2, 1921, the anniversary of the Balfour Declaration. The passage of more than a quarter of a century since that date has not dimmed the glow of the words with which Miss Szold impressed upon the young women her sense of the significance of the occasion:

> During all the days of preparation for this evening's exercises my thoughts, my emotions, my very steps hither and thither were attuned to one constant rhythm. The pregnant phrase of our liturgical poet who celebrates the Sabbath, kept running through my mind: "In execution the last, in thought the first." For this day *you* have waited three years, and across the ocean there are thousands of women who have waited for it nearly ten years. When they sent two pioneer nurses over here, to inaugurate District Visiting Nursing, they thought of this evening. When the summons came to enlarge the number of nurses from two to twenty, they rejoiced for the sake of this evening. When the summons required the addition of physicians to nurses, they thought that this circumstance would hasten the coming of this evening. When they had to wait for two years, until the passions of war permitted their expedition to enter the land, they consoled themselves with the thought that the completer preparation gave greater hope for the perfection of this evening. When, on the eve of departure of the

expedition, they received a letter from Dr. Kaghan, the only one received, though not the only one written, for over two years, which reported that an attempt had been made to start a Nurses Training Class, it was considered the best augury for the success of the expedition and a sure pledge of the coming of this evening. When the electric spark, three years ago today, flashed the news to America that the Rothschild Hospital had been re-opened in Jerusalem under the auspices of the American Zionist Medical Unit, they felt that this evening was already a reality. With them, though this evening in a sense is "the last in execution," it has always been "the first in thought." And tonight these thousands of women are thinking of you, my dear girls, with rejoicing in their hearts. They are full of envy of me that I am privileged to speak to you, face to face, within the boundaries of the land of hope, within the confines of the Holy City. I can almost hear their voices, thrilled with gratitude, say, as I now say with fervor, "Praised be God who has kept us alive and maintained us and permitted us to reach this day."

Early in the Zionist program came plans for a Hebrew University, in a sense the spiritual substitute for the Temple on whose ancient site of Mount Moriah the beautiful Moslem Dome of the Rock now stands. The University was to crown the heights of Mount Scopus; it was to be a symbol of light and learning, its portals open to all, with no quota system operating to exclude any of alien blood or creed. Since construction and growth would necessarily be slow, depending upon voluntary contributions from Jewry over a period of years, its initial departments would be those catering to the fundamental spiritual and practical needs of the community. A library; research laboratories for postgraduate study of tropical and subtropical diseases, and of animal and plant parasitology; departments for the study of Hebraic and Arabic literatures—these were considered the first essentials.

To Miss Szold and her associates in Hadassah the plans for the University opened up vistas for further service. Ultimately there would have to be a full department of medicine and a medical college for the education of young physicians. An essential part of the educational structure would be a well-equipped, modern hospital. Here was the Rothschild–Hadassah Hospital, functioning as a modern institution of healing. Why should it not become the Rothschild–Hadassah University Hospital?

Negotiations were entered upon with a body of American Jewish physicians who had independently expressed their desire to found a medical school, and the two organizations combined to bring their plans to fruition. May 9, 1939, saw the opening of the first departments of the million-dollar hospital building on Mount Scopus. Starting with 215 beds, an increase over the capacity of the Rothschild Hospital, the new institution made its plans for further increases to 300, then to 500 beds.

True to the original concept of the medical work as a non-charitable enterprise, Hadassah had early provided for a devolutionary program. In the first year of its establishment the patients attending the hospitals and clinics were able to pay only eight percent of total expenditure; during the fiscal year 1944-45, forty-three percent was covered by payments of the local population. Hospitals in Tel Aviv, Tiberias and Haifa were taken over either by the municipality or some other public body. So with other activities. The Rural Sick Benefit Fund of the Labor Organization took over the operation of forty-five rural dispensaries. Specialized health work, such as anti-tuberculosis, became the concern of volunteer local bodies.

To the Rothschild–Hadassah University Hospital (RHUH) was reserved the function of serving as a center for the scientific study of measures of diagnosis and therapy, for nursing education, medical education, research and the development of programs of preventive medicine. Its equipment and the quality of its personnel, including such world figures as Adler, Feigenbaum, Halberstaedter and Zondek, served to make it the model hospital for the entire Middle East area, with even wider scope for usefulness since war's destruction had left so few first-class medical research centers in operation east of London.

It has seemed desirable to give the foregoing sketch of Hadassah's medical activity in order to show its scope and quality. After her arrival in Palestine, in May, 1920, Miss Szold was closely associated with its direction, both as consultant and administrator. Even though she had no professional training, her handling of the recurrent problems—resignations, strikes, money difficulties, defects in organization and in work—won her the respect of the professional members of the Unit. The head nurse, resentful of the inclusion of a layman in discussions on matters of professional concern, testified later: "As my contacts with Miss Szold increased, I discovered that she knew a great deal about nursing, and as time went on I felt that there was not a phase of nursing education that she was not familiar with."

Others also learned, to their astonishment, that this particular layman was mistress of their problems. Dr. Rubinow left Palestine for a five-month absence during which Henrietta Szold was charged with the responsibility for a staff of some six hundred people, a dozen institutions, and a budget of more than a half-million dollars. There may have been a little surprise mingled with Dr. Rubinow's pleasure when he found, upon his return, that a layman who claimed no knowledge of hospital administration or of health work had kept the organization intact in his absence.

Most astonished of all were the physicians. Invited to make the opening address at a medical conference called to discuss the establishment of a faculty of medicine, Miss Szold asked one of the physicians for suggestions as to the subject of her talk. Accepting the subject he proposed, she indicated that the details he was about to give her on how to develop the subject, were unnecessary. Her presentation created a sensation. She pointed out to the physicians the futility of the development they had in mind. There was no point, she told them, in trying to develop this or that specialty as an independent unit without the support of related fields. Thus the gynecologist would need a heart specialist, the heart specialist required laboratories and so on. She sketched the budget problems that were involved in the proposed undertaking. The doctors listened agape while she expounded before them the interrelationships among the various fields of medicine with the clarity of one long conversant with problems of hospitalization.

In a letter written in 1920, she had said: "That the Unit was imperfect—that it is imperfect now—no one knows better than I; but when all its imperfections are summed up, there remains an achievement, attained in a period of less than two years, which in my judgment will be one of the bright spots in the history of the early reconstruction movement in Palestine. I am not very conversant with medical literature, but I have no hesitation in expressing my doubt whether any such big piece of constructive medical work has ever been done in a 'colony' even by the greatest imperialistic colonizing powers." And later: "Our medical undertaking was not unique in that it gave the country doctors—they could have come of themselves; in that we gave it nurses—they could have been brought in by one or another agency or many agencies; in that we gave it drugs and instruments—eventually they would have been purchased without us. Our distinction is that we established a system and a standard. They were the compelling force that wrung good work even from the mediocre. Such must be our objective in future, too. To depart from it means—decline from our Zionist ideal."

In one respect Miss Szold and the Hadassah Board considered their Palestinian program a failure. It was a keen disappointment that the plan for socialized medicine which they had expected to introduce fell through. Dr. Rubinow and Miss Szold fought long and hard to induce its acceptance. The opposition of the staff, seconded by organized labor whose philosophy might have been expected to welcome and foster the idea, proved too strong. The plan for socialized medicine was rejected finally and decisively. A few years later the Labor Organization adopted it for its own membership and succeeded in establishing a highly efficient system of medical service, including hospitals, clinics, and rest homes.

It is not within the scope of the present volume to trace, even briefly, the history of all the departments of work in the development of which Henrietta Szold acted as moving spirit, or administrator, or both. But it is impossible to ignore them completely. For even in the period of her absorption in the problems of the Unit, her mind was reaching out in other directions. In March, 1921, she was writing to her cousin, Mrs. Emil Weinheim: "Interests lie around loose here—in fact, they are heaped up at every corner and turn!"

One of these interests, the Nurses Training School, has been referred to in this chapter. Another, school hygiene, probably the most inclusive system in operation anywhere,* had its inception with the antitrachoma treatments begun by the first two nurses. The arrival of the Unit brought an intensification of anti-trachoma measures, the result being virtual eradication of the disease in the schools of the Jewish community.

Gradually the school hygiene work, under the enthusiastic direction of Dr. Berachyahu, was widened and deepened. For the ten years preceding the recent post-war immigration practically every child in school and kindergarten was under supervision. Not only did he receive a complete periodic examination, physical and psychological, but where called for, full medical treatment was supplied by the agencies of Hadassah—hospital, clinic and Straus Health Center. Preventive measures were taken, corrective exercises were given for physical defects and each case was carefully followed up.

Psychiatric testing began with kindergarten entrants, in the hope that the maladjustments of later years might be avoided. Here, likewise, treatment by a professional for as long as necessary, was an essential part of the service. Guidance clinics helped round out the system. In this service a staff of eighty to ninety physicians was engaged, full and part time, and some fifty nurses, all especially trained for their duties.

Among the early worries on Miss Szold's mind were the incidents of children fainting in their classrooms for lack

* This volume does not take into account the deterioration in services which necessarily followed the Arab-Jewish war of 1948 and the influx of sick and destitute Jewish refugees which has doubled the population.

of food. One of her visitors from America, Dr. Maurice Harris of Temple Israel in New York, placed in her hands a money gift from the children of his religious school, to be used for feeding the children of Palestine. Using the gift as a starter, she made it the agency for developing a social institution in Palestine. The pupils in all the Jewish religious schools in the United States were to be drawn into her program. They were to be asked for donations, but instead of giving the money outright, they were to buy flower seeds some six weeks before Shabuot (Pentecost), celebrated in Palestine as the Festival of the First Fruits, and plant the seeds in time to bring them to bloom for the celebration of the holiday. The planting and nurture of the seeds would keep the children in mind of their purpose. Their flowering, coinciding with the holiday, would establish a spiritual connection between them and the land of their fathers. The profits from the sale of the seeds were to provide the funds for school luncheons in Palestine.

In Palestine the educational aspect of the School Luncheons program was and is the teaching of cooking in the schools. A study of nutritive values and of balanced diet is included. Orderliness in food preparation, in the setting of the tables and in the serving of meals is insisted upon in communities habituated to slipshod food habits. Flowers and napkins add touches of grace much appreciated by the children. A sense of decorum is apparent in those who cook and serve and partake of the food. And the curse of charity has been removed, for payment is required of all but the most needy, the sums varying with the ability of the family to pay.

Even in the kindergartens the tots share in the work. They set and clear the tables and wait on their schoolmates. Cooking is taught in lower school grades, to boys as well as to girls, while in the upper grades dietetics is added and taught as a science on a level with academic subjects.

The educational aspect of the program was made possible by the advent of Mrs. Sarah Bavli, a dietitian whose training in Holland had been supplemented by study in the United States. Her capable hands have continued to guide and develop the work.

A related project, kept in abeyance by lack of funds, became a possibility much later through the generosity of the Esco Foundation Fund* for Palestine. The gift enabled Miss Szold to make a start at setting right a situation that cried for attention—the need for systematic training in cooking in the agricultural settlements. In the settlements intense interest in the production of food was not accompanied by a corresponding interest in its proper preparation for the table. Good raw materials brought into the kitchens were carried into the dining rooms, lacking in taste and with nutritive values impaired. The contemptuous attitude of the parents toward kitchen work carried over to the children. At one settlement the teachers called on the School Luncheons Committee for advice. The children refused to finish their food, took dislikes to dishes, called a strike when spinach appeared on the table. When appealed to not to waste food, they poked fun at the "registration of left-overs."

Questions both of health and of pedagogy were involved. The appeal to the School Luncheons Committee brought the advice to teach cooking, and the offer of cooperation. Objections were raised by the parents. The teaching of cooking, they said, was a waste of time. It was bad enough

* Esco Foundation Fund for Palestine—A private fund established by Frank and Ethel Silverman Cohen for initiating special projects in or for Palestine, not otherwise provided for.

that they, the parents, had to put in their time in the kitchen. They refused their cooperation and persuaded the settlement to withhold financial assistance for the project.

Notwithstanding the objections, the teachers went ahead. Dangling the idea of self-help before the children, and of emulation of their parents' pioneering experiences, they succeeded in winning them over. The inadequate equipment—all the water had to be carried in—made the children feel that they were participating in pioneer living. Each little improvement, introduced by themselves, was a triumph. The children's "Kitchen Committee" assumed responsibility for supplies, menus, budgets. The food they themselves cooked was wonderful! "All dishes now are eaten," reported the teachers, "including even spinach, the war on which has ceased, and a quiet and pleasant atmosphere reigns in the dining room."

Miss Szold wrote her thanks to the Esco Foundation: "To be the instrument for filling so fundamental a need promises a wealth of pleasant, stimulating experiences, new ones, leading into fields and opening vistas of knowledge closed to me hitherto. Untrodden fields, newly revealed vistas—at seventy-five—that is romance!"

Certainly there were no gaping voids in her time that begged to be filled, but other interests forced themselves into crannies of her days and nights. This was the period that saw the beginning of Miss Szold's struggle (treated in a later chapter) to weld the Jewish women of Palestine into a body which would organize and develop modern social service in the community—a task made difficult by the opposition of groups whose staunch social doctrines made them contemptuous of "ameliorative" measures.

An attempt, involving much time and effort, to bring together all the women of Palestine—Christians, Moslems and Jews—came to nothing. It was not possible to bring the Moslem women of Palestine out of their retirement into the world of every-day affairs. A contributing reason may have been fear by missionary organizations of the influence of Henrietta Szold's personality. Miss Szold was aware of the feeling: "Recently the fiat has gone forth that I am to be boycotted!* I am somewhat in the position of Alice Seligsberg, against whom Mrs. —— warned some of her friends with the caution: "She is too intelligent."

Miss Szold's personal life during the twenties was made smooth and pleasant by the companionship and home-making talents of Sophia Berger (later Mrs. E. N. Mohl) with whom she shared a simple, tastefully furnished home. At Sophia's insistence there were occasional breaks in the routine of work—attendance at concerts of the Jerusalem String Quartet, holiday visits to the Dead Sea, moonlight walks in the Old City and sunset suppers on its walls, out-door picnic lunches on the glorious mornings of winter and spring.

Mrs. Mohl will never forget their visit to Ramallah during the Shabuot season; Miss Szold was fascinated when she saw enacted in real life the harvest customs described in the *Book of Ruth*—the coming of the women from across Jordan for the harvesting of the barley, just as Naomi came with Ruth; the call from a housetop, announcing that there would be no reaping for two weeks; the eating of the Arabic *kali*, the "parched corn" of the Ruth story. Here, as always, Henrietta's interest in botany came to the fore. On a tiny bit of ground, marked out by the handkerchief she spread over it, she counted forty-nine varieties of field growth.

In the course of this visit Miss Szold was invited to speak to the older boys of the school—a Christian school maintained by the Friends—on Jewish work in Palestine. She

* See page 107.

began her talk by telling them of her trip to Hungary as a young woman. She had gone, knowing all about her kinsfolk because her parents had spoken frequently of their home and their families. Her kinsfolk did not know her or the America she had come from. Then she drew a parallel between her visit to Hungary and the coming of the Jew to Palestine, where his Arab cousins were living. The Jew was strange to the language and the customs of the Arabs, yet he knew Palestine because he knew the Bible, he had carried it with him for two thousand years. The Arabs did not know their Jewish cousin, did not know the land, the many lands, from which he came, and therefore could not understand him. "If I felt so drawn to my cousins' home that I wanted to establish myself there, would I drive my cousins out—the very ones who have carried on some of the traditions I love? Or would I enlarge and beautify the house, with all the knowledge I had gathered in America?"

The Jew had lived in his history as in a home, she went on. He had lived in the past—though, in point of fact, he had *not* lived in the home his past had made; he had only dreamed in it. He could not live according to his convictions and his laws because he did not control all the conditions of life, particularly its political conditions. But the three-fold cord of history, made up of his religion, his law, his literature, was too strong to be broken. This was what Balfour* had understood. This was the reason for the Balfour Declaration—an opportunity given, not a land given. The Arab and the Jew had worked together in the Middle Ages. She hoped they would be able to work together again. A Semitic Federation might be the goal for both.

Miss Szold invited the boys to ask questions. One of the boys arose and stated that the Jews could not be forgiven

* See page 96.

because they had desecrated Christian churches and holy places during the war (World War I); Miss Szold's denial was vehement. There had not been a single case of desecration of Christian holy places by Jews, she asserted. On the contrary, synagogues and Jewish cemeteries had been wantonly destroyed. "You, a Christian, ought to go down on your knees and beg my forgiveness for destruction wrought by Christians on Jewish synagogues and holy places!" Her hostess attempted to excuse the Arabs on the ground of their ignorance. Her answer was: "Ignorance is also a crime."

7. *Palestine Zionist Executive*

"What I have done is not to work, not to construct"

IN THE middle 20's the situation in Palestine was one of crisis. A period of rapid expansion in immigration and colonization, involving at times a rash expenditure of uncollected funds, had brought the finances of the World Zionist Organization to a point where its legitimate commitments could no longer be met. Decreasing collections from world Jewry, particularly from America, with consequent difficulties in meeting salaries and other expenses, made the period one of constant strain.

Miss Szold traveled to the Zionist Congress of 1927 with other delegates. She spent her time on board reading and discussing letters, reports, newspaper items, and all sorts of documents bearing on the Congress issues. She was convinced that the whole Zionist world was profoundly disturbed about the situation in Palestine and the methods of work there. She wondered whether the Congress would be able to produce plans and the men to execute them: "For such a result the other delegates must have more constructive notions than I can boast of."

When she found herself made one of a Palestine Executive Committee of three—the others were Harry Sacher and Colonel Frederick H. Kisch, both of England—she found it regrettable that at that critical juncture the great

Zionist movement had no one better to turn to than a tired old woman of sixty-seven.

Miss Szold's particular responsibilities on the Executive were to be health and education. Expansion and construction activities were no longer possible. Her capacity for building up, for laying a foundation stone by stone, could not be exercised. She was obliged to turn her talents to conserving—or more exactly, to restricting and retrenching; a retrenchment which added to the already large numbers of unemployed, bringing them to twenty percent of the population.

Funds were so short that there was no money on hand even to transfer the unemployed of Tel Aviv and establish them in settlements where they were needed. The Jordan Valley had suffered a drought and the settlers there were hungry. Teachers' salaries were in arrears—arrears that were to pile up to seven months—and the teachers were on strike. Kindergartens had to be given up where they could not be maintained privately by parents; the upper grades of the high schools and the first years of the teachers' seminaries were closed down; there was not even money for the purchase of chalk. The Palestinian Director of Education gave up his task in despair. Dr. I. B. Berkson, an American educator, was installed to succeed him, but blocked by lack of funds, he was unable to concentrate on pedagogic problems.

In America, factionalism had lost the Zionist Organization some of its most influential adherents (not, however, their loyalty to Zionism)—among others, Supreme Court Justice Louis D. Brandeis and Federal Judge Julian W. Mack, two of Miss Szold's warmest supporters. The letters Miss Szold addressed to the American organization, giving detailed reports on the situation in Palestine, remained unanswered and apparently unnoted. Factionalism left little time for attention to problems of growth or retrenchment in Palestine.

After she had struggled for months to keep the schools open on a budget cut from L75,000 to L55,000, a gift of $20,000 from Junior Hadassah enabled Miss Szold to reopen some of the kindergartens. Then Baron Edmond de Rothschild came to her assistance with $25,000. An editorial inaccuracy in connection with the Baron's gift aroused her anger: "Can you picture to yourselves how I felt when I saw your publicity stunt in putting Baron Rothschild's picture on the cover page of *The New Palestine* with the legend of $90,000 for education? You know by this time that the gift was only $25,000. I wish the person who devised that publicity stunt could sit at my desk and shift and shift and shift small sums like L2 and L3 from page to page of the budget for education, in order to make it possible to open one school after the other. Why, they are asking for money for chalk and I haven't it to give to them! Can't you see that my method of telling the truth is the proper one, even from the propaganda point of view? Can't you understand that when the false report goes to all sections of the country, Zionists will draw a deep breath and rejoice, instead of getting down to work? While you have sent us here to be stern twenty-four hours of the day, you follow the line of least resistance. You have deserted the Executive of your choice . . . I cannot let denunciation stand as my last word. In good Jewish fashion, I must add friendly greetings. But—!"

Her bitterness is directed particularly against the American associates who had persuaded her to accept the post of responsibility. Fourteen months of acute misery were poured into words expressing the personal hurt: "Before I left America . . . my friends in the Zionist world expressed their appreciation of my sacrifice in coming here at this juncture. They knew that I considered my coming here at this time the only sacrifice I had ever made. Not only did I know how hopeless the situation was; I also had little confidence in my own ability to cope with it or any phase of it. I was especially timid about the financial and economic problems that were naturally pushed to the foreground. I doubted my ability to make any contribution to the solution of such problems even in normal times, let alone in times of trouble and doubt. The friends who expressed their appreciation of my sacrifice . . . gave me, in public and in private, the assurance that personally I should receive their support. . . .

"The fourteen months I have been here—no, I refuse to tell you what they have been. I cannot calmly write the details. Not only has it been work from eighteen to twenty hours without cease, but it has been a self-denial in work itself such as I have never experienced. Let me explain that phrase. I have been accustomed all my life to work. What I have done here is to resist. What I have done and what my associates have done throughout the year is not to work, not to construct. We have strained every nerve to pay for the joy of creation which our predecessors indulged in. They carried projects into effect, and we are paying the piper. . . .

"After more than a generation of Zionist work in America, I confess I do not see how, at the end of my term in September of this year, I can go back to America and again associate myself with those with whom I have worked for so many years, be they within the Organization or be they in the 'Opposition'. I am almost prepared to believe that with the end of my term of office here will end my connection with Zionism, [and] that not because I despair of Palestine, and not because I despair of Zionist Organizations, but because I have been wounded too deeply by those whose personal attachment was sanctified for me by their interest in the ideals that gave direction to my own life."

On the other hand her tribute of gratitude goes out to Field-Marshal Lord Plumer, then High Commisioner,* whose sympathy and active cooperation helped the country over some difficult situations. His query at their first interview: "Does not the Government share the responsibility with the Zionist Organization?" indicated a point of view not always to be found in government circles. He made the impression upon Miss Szold of an unusually upright administrator whose sense of right was inflexible, but whose administrative rigidity was tempered by humane sympathies. Her interview with him left her both stimulated and soothed.

Professor Norman Bentwich, then Chief Justice in the Palestine Government, recalls meetings of the Executive Council of the Government at which Henrietta Szold presented the requests of the Palestine Zionist Executive: "She was nearing her seventieth year; Lord Plumer had just attained it. The two veterans were inspired with an equal devotion to the land and its peoples. While the country was tranquil, the Jewish population passed through a difficult period because of the economic crisis in Europe. For a time the Yishuv was faced with serious unemployment. That was just the difficulty Henrietta Szold was made to tackle, and she and Lord Plumer fitted like hand to glove in concerting measures of constructive relief." The building of the beautiful archaeological museum with money donated by the Rockefeller Foundation, and the dredging of Haifa Harbor to give approach to sea-going vessels were among the products of the Government's cooperation.

* Served 1925-28.

One of the government officials with whom she negotiated marvelled at the effect of Miss Szold's personality on others, in particular at her power to jack others up to her own level. To a rather flippant under-officer in the government education department she said: "If you want to be cynical, of course you can, but I assume the government wants to help." She frequently succeeded in making her point where other Zionist officials failed.

It was during her conduct of school affairs that she wrested from the government a grant-in-aid of L20,000, the first substantial grant ever made by the government to Jewish education. The fact that Jews were supplying by far the larger share of government income—although they were only eighteen percent of the population they were paying fifty to sixty percent of the taxes—had not entitled them to the usual benefits of taxation. That same taxation, however, was providing full support for the Arab schools at about ten times the rate allowed for the Jewish schools. Miss Szold's presentation before the government of the educational needs of the country included those of the Arabs as well as those of the Jews. The largeness of her stature, her tendency to view the needs of the country as a whole, would permit no other treatment.

In addition to her budget difficulties, Miss Szold ran into other problems. She had long maintained that the education of the children was false; she had spoken of the political quarrels of the children in the kindergartens. With unification as her goal, she could not reconcile herself to the tri-partite system of education prevailing in the country. Three separate school systems—center, Labor left, and Orthodox right, each maintaining control not only over curriculum but over administration as well—did not gibe with her ideas on pedagogy. Her opposition to the party system in education created conflicts, particularly with the Mizrachi, right wing of the World Zionist Organization. At the next Congress, that of 1929, she was moved to state: "I am religious and Jewish myself, but I do not believe in the rule of priests. School children must not be drawn into religious strife."

Miss Szold's judgment characterized the two-year period as a heroic one. It was true that the discharging of debts was not a romantic, heart-lifting task. There was no glowing satisfaction in denying to the workers the possibility of carrying out their plans for houses, barns, stables, water installations, stock, seeds, implements. But in the self-denial imposed by untoward circumstances, she saw moral triumph—a hardening and stiffening of spiritual fiber. And there were positive results. The unemployment crisis had been weathered, doles were no longer being paid, the country needed more workers and the way had been paved for a new wave of immigration. Teachers' claims had been satisfied, progress had been made in establishing settlements more firmly on their economic foundations, and the debts of the Organization were reduced by one-third.

Strangely enough, in spite of long years of Zionist activity in America, in spite of her residence in Palestine and preoccupation with its affairs, Miss Szold's personality was, until the time of her service on the Palestine Executive, little known to the general public in Palestine. Outside of a circle of friends who valued her at her worth, the attitude toward her had been more or less one of tolerance. She was an amiable, missionary-minded lady interested in good works, particularly in hospital service for the poor. She was a magnet for money and in that capacity highly acceptable, but philanthropic activity was not to the taste of the socialist hierarchy that governed the political thinking of much of the community. Her election to the Executive had been bitterly opposed by the labor groups, and the article in their press which greeted her arrival after the election was a fierce attack on her ability and her preparation for the task.

In the two years, 1927-29, Jewish Palestine made a discovery: it discovered Henrietta Szold. When, after having been re-elected to office in 1929, she made known her decision to resign, there arose a cry of protest from all elements. The teachers issued a special number of their publication in her honor, paying tribute to her personality and her achievements. Although they were the ones who had suffered most bitterly through the failure of publicly collected funds, they had become her staunch supporters. At the end of one of their meetings with her, one of them was heard to murmur: "If she should ask for money from us, I think we would give it to her."

At the age of 6

Dr Benjamin Szold (father) at 60

At the age of 14

Courtesy Hadassah

Courtesy Hadassah

1899: Henrietta, Adele, Mother, Bertha, Rachel Szold

Courtesy Hadassah

As a young teacher, in Baltimore, in the 1880's

Courtesy Hadassah

In New York, during editorship of Jewish Publication Society, about 1910

Henrietta Szold's "Doodling"

Courtesy Hadassah

...e said. For the rest, I submerge myself in
...left the Vaad Leumi, which means that
...ible for the organization of the social
...any one else. The Vaad Leumi hasn't the
guts to appoint any one. I gave them warning of my resignation a year and a half before it took effect. So the remna-
and spirit of what I effected in the course of eight years is
vanishing into thin air. I kept on with the practical social
work in the Kehillah. I shall probably have to leave that, too,
very soon, because I cannot fit myself into a system built
up entirely on political partisanship. On the other hand the Youth
Aliyah has rushed in impetuously and has more than filled the inter-
stices on which I had counted for ordinary human intercourse and a
modicum of reading, both of which I have been deprived of these
many years. As a matter of fact the demands of the Youth Aliyah
upon time and strength by far exceed my diminished powers.

I had expected to go to Amsterdam to be present at the Youth Aliyah
Conference. My sisters — you know that they have been with me since
Pesach — were to accompany me, Adele to return to America, Bertha to
come back here with me. A week ago my sister Bertha suffered a
sudden collapse. I do not dare put on paper what we feared. She
is not out of danger. The physician is satisfied with her progress.
All our reservations were cancelled. It has been a week of great strain.
We haven't made any plans. At any rate she will be many
weeks before she can leave the bed.

I hope all goes well with you and your sisters. My fond
love to you.

Affectionately, Henrietta Szold

From a letter written by Henrietta Szold to Rose Zeitlin

8. *Social Welfare*

"Everything is chaotic and the chaos is static"

MISS SZOLD'S two years as a member of the Palestine Zionist Executive had wrought changes in the relations between her and her American friends. Bent on strengthening the young Jewish community, on making it self-dependent administratively, she had broken with her own immediate past: she no longer placed emphasis on close American administrative control over American-collected funds. She had advocated American control over the Hadassah Medical Organization in order to ensure the maintenance of standards. Now she saw that system as crippling the normal growth of the Palestine community and preventing the strengthening of the local forces. The bonds of absentee management would have to be thrown off; for example, the directorship of the Hadassah Medical Organization should be turned over to the Palestinians.

When the Zionist Congress of 1929 convened, it brought into being a new body, known as the Jewish Agency. The Agency was designed to draw into Palestinian work non-Zionist Jews who, although interested in cultural activities in Palestine and in developing the country as a refuge, did not accept the basic Zionist objective—a Jewish state.

Although she was voted into office as a member of the Jewish Agency, Miss Szold found that the attitude of the Zionist officials toward her was not conducive to good work or to good feeling. Opposition had been aroused in Orthodox circles by her criticism of the tri-partite system of education in Palestine. Moreover, the non-Zionists in the Agency held views on American control of American funds for Palestine which were not in consonance with her new orientation. Her participation in Zionist affairs was not encouraged; she was not even notified of meetings. Nevertheless she presented herself before the head of the Zionist Organization and made it clear that she was willing to work. But the only work the Organization wanted of her, she found, was to have her speak in public—and that she refused to do.

Miss Szold had stood for office in spite of an earlier determination not to accept election, not to return to Palestine. "Circumstances overruled me," she said. "But since the election took place, I realize that even my election is not an unalterable fact." Finding herself excluded from the responsibilities that went with office, she presented her resignation. It was accepted.

Her seventieth birthday was celebrated in America. The public meetings and addresses made her feel, she said, like a bubble filled not even with gas, but with that "inspirational" fluid she was expected to give out all the time.

She escaped from the round of festivities long enough to enjoy a motor trip with her sisters through the Shenandoah Valley southward to Charleston, South Carolina. She recorded that the snow was twenty-six inches high, and went on: "I have not measured the height of the piles of mail, nor have I counted the letters and cables I received. I simply set to work. I couldn't—I needn't tell you—have a card of thanks printed. Whether or not personality had been put into the messages and greetings, for me, the recipient, personality shone through, and I simply accepted the penalty of having reached the age of seventy in an atmosphere impregnated with publicity. Don't put the wrong construction on this cynical expression. Just as personality shone through for me from the most commonplace message, so I felt keenly, humbly, and gratefully, also the affection that prompted celebrations, public though they were. The upshot is that for six weeks I have been saying 'Thank ye, my ladies and my lords,' in a thousand variations."

The celebrations, however, did not mark out a path of work. But Palestine was beckoning her back. Within the framework of the Mandate Government the Jewish community had developed its own governmental organization. It consisted of an *Asefat Ha-Nivharim* (Elected Assembly) which at its annual meeting elected a *Vaad Leumi* (National Council). The *Vaad Leumi* in its turn chose from among its members an Executive Committee of seven. It was the function of this Executive Committee to administer the internal affairs of the Jewish community in the departments of politics, finance, education, health, social welfare, religious affairs, and cultural activities.

The Women's Party had headed its slate for the *Vaad Leumi* with her name, and the Labor Party—the same that had greeted her first election to the Palestine Zionist Executive with derision—was now yielding up one of its three precious seats on the Executive in order to make room for Henrietta Szold.

The invitation to return was not an easy solution to her problem: "It is not my absence that halts the work . . . I can see how impossible it would be to get such men as ——— and ——— immersed in National Council discussions, down to prosaic details . . . Everybody says the only thing to do is to go on with what we are doing, but it appears when they say it, they think only of the big, indefinite things—money-raising, colonization, education, etc. When I say it, I mean that everyone should continue doing intensively what was entrusted to him. But I am sure I couldn't get anyone to cooperate with me."

The period of indecision continued. Her faculties, active and unimpaired, made the prospect of inactivity intolerable. The letters written at this time express her indecision:

> My mind is a blank on my future.
>
> I cannot make up my mind where to spend the balance of my days, in America or in Palestine.
>
> What is my decision about myself? I am no farther than I was last April.
>
> Another twenty-four hours to fight with myself. I am finding it difficult beyond words to decide to go back, but I am finding it equally difficult to adjust myself to contemporary life in America. I can't see myself at work here fruitfully.

Nevertheless she remained more than moderately busy. "You will wonder why," she wrote, "sans position, sans responsibility, sans post, I am so busy that I can't do what I want. I wonder too. I am at the mercy of any and all with a grievance, a grief, or an idea."

Finally the call to align herself with a definite task proved decisive: "In Palestine they seem to think I can do a definite piece of organization work. So I go back." The reception there was, according to her own report, messianic. "My coming meant, according to some, the beginning of real work; according to others, the completion of the work; some expected me to solve all public problems; others, to find a solution for their private woes and troubles. After subtracting all these 'interested' parties there remained, I cannot but say, a large group of friends who were just glad to welcome me back. Some of them came down from Jerusalem and all the way to the vessel lying at anchor outside Jaffa; some met me as I disembarked at Jaffa, many crowded into my room at the hotel when I reached Jerusalem, and there has been a steady flow of them since."

Miss Szold landed in Palestine at the end of May, 1931. Her task was to be the planning of a method of transferring health and education activities from the World Zionist Executive to the Palestinian community. It became instead the establishment of a new department—Social Welfare.

"What do you think of my temerity in undertaking such a task?" she wrote. "When I came to Palestine I acted as though I were an expert on medical affairs. Fate made me pretend to be an expert on educational affairs in 1927. And now, in 1931, having passed the Psalmist's term of years, I dare go into another field in which to expertize is imperative."

The temerity was not so brazen as might appear at first sight, for the subject itself was not new to her. Before she had reached her twentieth birthday, her considered views on system and organization in welfare work had found expression in print. In 1880, writing in *The Jewish Messenger,* she pleaded for unification in the handling of charity funds, in order to do away with overlapping activities and thereby eliminate wastefulness.

Later the Jewish social workers in America turned to Henrietta Szold for help in one of their problems. Constant appeals were coming to Jewry in America from institutions and individuals in Palestine. There was no way of knowing which of the appeals for support deserved an answer in the affirmative. At the suggestion of Dr. Judah Magnes, the social workers requested Miss Szold to make a study of Palestine charitable institutions. For a period of two years she worked, sending out questionnaires, collecting, scrutinizing and organizing her data. In 1912 she presented her findings before the National Conference of Jewish Charities. A haphazard charity system, she reported, had made for the development of evils. Collections were loosely supervised both at source and at destination, thereby encouraging irresponsibility among administrators and pauperization among recipients. Her suggestion then was that the study be continued on a permanent basis. She recommended specifically that a responsible body be established to supervise all charitable enterprises, and that an auditing system be introduced. Her later colleagues in social work in Palestine never knew of this page out of her past, but they will hardly be surprised to learn of it.

No sooner did she arrive in Palestine in 1920 than she tackled the problem of social welfare work. She found an American associate, Bathsheba Kesselman (Mrs. Robert Kesselman) already on the ground, engaged in a struggle to organize the Jewish women of the country for child and maternity care. Mrs. Kesselman lost no time in drawing Miss Szold into the work.

It was a situation that taxed all Miss Szold's patience. Later she recalled the first meeting—women newly arrived from Europe. Sephardic women in their lace headcloths, pantalooned Yemenites, wimpled Bokharans in brilliant silks, a "Babel that was supposed to be a discussion of purpose and method." The task again, as it had been in Hadassah, was two-fold, each purpose acting on the other. It was to develop a practical piece of social work to be carried out by the women. Their participation in that work would teach them to understand its problems and to devise ways of dealing with them: working on those problems would develop their sense of personal responsibility toward the community.

The women pleaded inexperience. She answered them: "My work is academic—teaching, editing. I would much rather be a teacher. But now I *must* do this. This is your present duty. You *are* able to do the work." Nor was she content to draw upon the European intelligentsia only. At her insistence the ranks of the Sephardim and the Yemenites and the ultra-orthodox Europeans were made to yield their quota of forces ready to act and to learn.

Funds being necessarily small at the outset, emphasis was laid on personal service—regular visits to the homes of pregnant women to instruct them in hygiene and to introduce them to the infant welfare stations of Hadassah. For the first time, also, there was introduced in Palestine a system of social statistics, kept by the volunteer workers. Many were shaken out of their complacency on learning that the pay earned by fathers of families—and many families were large—ran from 1½ to 2 piastres a day (at that time a piastre equalled five cents), on those days when work was to be found. These earnings were supplemented by begging and by doles paid out of Zionist funds, but the Zionist institutions did nothing to correct the basic situation.

The most difficult feature of Miss Szold's task was to make the members understand that she was not going to secure the money for the work from America. She insisted that the members themselves must raise their funds locally and must content themselves with doing what they could pay for: "My triumph is that I do nothing—the committee must do everything, under my direction. But it's like holding in wild horses. They have wanted to jump when they did not know how to crawl. And the chief lesson I have carried home is a cooperation with the agencies that actually exist."

One other ultimate purpose was inherent in her plan. This band of women, augmented in number and strengthened by experience, would become, she hoped, an independent, central body to which Jewish women's organizations everywhere in the world would turn for guidance in planning work for Palestine. With them as consultants, new programs would be charted; through them new projects would be brought into being. Unfortunately this larger aspect of her plan ended in failure—a failure to be laid squarely at the door of the Women's International Zionist Organization (Wizo), centered in London, which preferred to make of the Palestinian organization a mere branch of the world body, rather than grant it the dignity of independent status and the authority which were envisioned for it by its founder.

In her efforts to bring order into the welter of public welfare activities, Henrietta Szold made repeated attempts to enlist the two large Diaspora organizations—the Wizo, mentioned above, and the American Hadassah. Twice she traveled to London to present her carefully thought-out plans. Reviewing the conference of June, 1930, Miss Szold wrote:

"And why did I go to London? First, I suppose, because I am a fool and, second, because I hoped to be able to influence the women to take a wider view of their duty toward Palestine. I accepted the invitation because I hoped for an opportunity to urge the acceptance of the large plan I have been cherishing for years—that the Zionist women make themselves responsible for the non-economic interests; that is, Health, Education, and Social Service. In principle the idea was accepted. It will be more than a year and a day before its execution is even begun. There are real difficulties in the plan itself, and still greater difficulties growing out of the inertia of the European women, and even greater ones out of the powers that be, vested in our lords and masters. Now am I or am I not a fool?"

Her forebodings proved well founded. She wrote soon afterwards of the mad journey she had made in the hope that she could put a big idea in the heads of the women. During the discussions she thought she was succeeding. After she left other forces played upon the Wizo and carried the day. Her plan to coordinate the women's work had failed.

Now, in 1931, Miss Szold's recall to Palestine brought her again face to face with problems of construction and coordination. She characterized the situation as monstrous: "Everything is chaotic and the chaos is static." Social work was looked down upon as the successor to charity, but everyone continued to do charity in the antiquated way.

To Ruth Cohen, a social worker in America, Miss Szold enumerated the special difficulties—vested interests, traditions, heterogeneous population, prejudices, helter-skelter attempts to relieve this or that particular problem and, especially, complete lack of understanding that money was needed for administration. For actual social service, funds were pitifully small. The city of Haifa permitted the expenditure of L20 monthly: that sum had to suffice to provide help to transients, care for children, food for the hungry, clothing for the naked, housing for the roofless, the securing of work for the unemployed, granting of loans and care of the sick.

She confided to Miss Cohen her conception of the qualifications of an effective social worker: "I am following the developments of social work, particularly in the

United States and in Germany, with some glimpses of France, England and Geneva. Day after day my amazement grows at the development in the course of less than a generation of this new profession of the social worker. There is not a single department of our complex life in this tortured universe of ours that the social worker can afford to pass by indifferently. His effectiveness depends upon his ability to keep himself *au courant* with the progress of applied science, political happenings, social theories, psychology, and biologic thought, not to mention business, education, and health. And unless there comes a touch of philosophy, that is, thinking, to cement together information that flows through all these channels, all the rest avails naught.

"What appals me is that in the nature of things I cannot possibly live long enough to see the results of my labors crystallizing into an organism. It is disconcerting. During the last few weeks two prominent Jewish social service workers from Germany have been here and we arranged discussions with them. They were most interesting, most instructive, and again I must use the word, most disconcerting. I found myself wishing that they would lose their jobs in Germany and come to Palestine and take my place."

Soon after this her wishes were realized and the professional social workers came pouring in from Germany. They were swept in on the tide that threw a new wave of immigration up on the shores of Palestine literally as well as figuratively, for the beaches of Tel Aviv became sleeping quarters for whole families.

Miss Szold struggled unremittingly and for the most part without avail to make the *Vaad Leumi* understand its responsibility for a budget. The funds that came to her personally from America were put by her to social welfare uses which were rightly, she felt, the responsibility of the local community. It did not add to her serenity to feel, as she sometimes did, that the invitation she had received to come to Palestine had been partly motivated by a recognition of her power to attract gifts of money from the United States. She struggled on, established a school for training professional social workers and, with money from the American Esco, she set up a boys' village—a farming community for neglected children and young delinquents on probation.

In his article, *Principles of Social Work in Palestine according to Henrietta Szold,* Dr. Alexander Dushkin, Professor of Education, puts forward the thesis that it was fortunate for Palestine that the initiation of organized social work was put into the hands of Henrietta Szold. The advantages he saw in that choice rather than in the choice of a professional were her experience as a communal leader and the wide range of her social activity over a long period of years. He might have mentioned a third point—her vision.

According to Dr. Dushkin, the structure raised by Henrietta Szold rested on three principles. The first principle itself had a three-pillared basis—first, education, necessary for integrating the young into the life and civilization of the community; second, health, to restore to normal functioning those incapacitated by sickness or accident; third, social welfare, for the transformation of the poverty-stricken, the undernourished, the neglected, the delinquent, the maladjusted, into an independent, productive citizenry.

Her second basic principle, Dr. Dushkin states, was her approach to the work. She refused to look upon it as in any sense negative, and rejected vigorously the use of such terms as "non-productive" to designate "such tingling human activities as are conveyed by the headings health, education and social service. For if taking industrial raw materials and working them into useful forms was considered productive, how much more should the shaping of human raw material be so considered. "Non-economic" was the term she preferred.

The third principle was the centering of social welfare work in the family. Family case work, hitherto overlooked in Palestine, was to be basic, not the problems of the individual looked after by this or that specialized institution.

The ultimate objective of all social welfare work was legislation: for this final goal the development of public opinion was essential. To this end the professional social worker had to keep in mind, as one of his primary functions, the development of volunteer groups. These groups, working as aids to the professionals, might do much to bring before the general public and before government circles the conclusions to which their experience had led them.

The Mandatory Government had been blissfully oblivious of the need for social legislation. Of its own accord it had made no move. There was no compulsory education law. In the Arab and in the Oriental Jewish communities superfluous female offspring were frequently married off, by sale, at the age of ten or eleven. Under pressure from the League of Jewish Women for Equal Rights, the Government had introduced a law prohibiting the marriage of any girl under fifteen years of age. Girls of seven and eight worked long hours in households only slightly more prosperous than their own. Very young children were sent out on the streets to beg, shine shoes, run errands. When they got into trouble with the law, they received the punishment justly due their elders. Treatment for the delinquent consisted of flogging and imprisonment. The British probation officer neither spoke nor understood the language of the Jewish boys. Conviction for a trifling offense meant a term in a reformatory in the company of older boys some of whom had been consigned for murder.

Despite the inertia of the government, Miss Szold's work brought distinct advances. Within a few years thirteen was set as the lowest working age; though the regulation was largely disregarded, it meant something to have it on the government books. For those under sixteen, seven hours was fixed as a maximum day. The first probation officer of the government, appointed in 1933, two years after Miss Szold began work, was superseded later by one with modern professional training. In 1944 the government established its own Department of Social Welfare, using on its staff young people from the Jerusalem school for training social workers, established by Miss Szold.

In spite of the difficulties which beset her, it was possible for her to report progress. The annual conference for the discussion of social welfare questions showed a growing response from the community. Attendance grew from fifteen in the first conference to sixty in the second, one hundred and twenty in the third, and over three hundred in the fourth. The fact that there were many men among them, and that many of the delegates were from the ranks of the Labor Party, proved that the welfare program was winning recognition as a piece of socially constructive work. It was to this Labor Party she had earlier made reference when she said: "The Histadruth does not want its aristocrats to sit on the same bench with my proletarians."

The Zionist Congress of 1935 also brought a glow of satisfaction. Miss Szold had intended to report only on

Youth Aliyah,* which she had been directing since 1933. She told of her visits to the Palestinian settlements where the youth from Germany were being cared for. Suddenly she saw an opportunity to do something for social welfare; she launched into an account of the inhumanities practised against Jewish children in other times and at other places. She reminded her audience of Edgar Mortara, baptized by a priest smuggled into the parents' home by a Catholic nurse, later seized by the Church, reared in a monastery and dedicated to the priesthood; of the children torn from their parents' arms by the Inquisition and transported to the newly-discovered Isle of St. Thomas, few of them surviving the rigors of the journey; of the children of Russia snatched for recruitment in the army. Then she charged her hearers with crime—the crime of failing to meet the primary needs of the children of Palestine's slums, next to immigration the most important problem of the community. Her eloquence won the grant of a budget, although only one third of the amount requested. Nevertheless, the fact that the claim was recognized as just was a long step forward.

Later, speaking before a group of welfare workers in New York, Miss Szold recounted the story of her social service in Palestine. How had she become a specialist, they wanted to know, in so many departments. "We are specialists," they said, "in this, or that, or another phase of work. Each of us has spent a lifetime mastering his particular field. How is it that you have succeeded in becoming an expert in so many fields?" "You work with your intellect," was her answer. "My work is that of a mother who must watch out for her children's wants and for their future. The people of Palestine are my children, and I feel like the mother who must be on the lookout for symptoms of

* See Chapters 13-17 inclusive.

illnesses and provide against them. My work, like the mother's, comes from the heart."

Hers was not the heart of the over-indulgent mother who cannot see weaknesses and errors. While explaining spiritual inadequacies by the heritage of an unhappy past and a stormy present, she did not excuse these inadequacies. She condemned the lack of cohesion she saw, the love of pleasure, the aggressiveness. "We need," she said, "either a great spiritual leader or, in lieu of him, an educational system that will lead us step by step upward."

In 1938 Miss Szold resigned her post as head of the Social Welfare Department. She had struggled for eight years to establish and maintain a service, without funds for what she considered the barest essentials—administrative needs, investigations, experimental undertakings, interpretation of statistics, case work, clerical help for volunteer workers. She hoped that those who came after her would succeed where she felt that she had failed.

9. *Jew, Arab, Briton—1920-29*

"Action as against talk and right action as against wrong"

ON NOVEMBER 2, 1917, the document known as the Balfour Declaration had been issued. It took the form of a letter from Arthur James Balfour, Britain's Prime Minister, addressed to Lord James de Rothschild:

> I have much pleasure in conveying to you on behalf of His Majesty's Government the following declaration of sympathy with the Jewish Zionist aspirations, which has been submitted to and approved by the Cabinet.
>
> His Majesty's Government view with favor the establishment in Palestine of a National Home for the Jewish people, and will use their best endeavors to facilitate the achievement of this object, it being clearly understood that nothing shall be done which may prejudice the civil and religious rights of existing non-Jewish communities in Palestine, or the rights and political status enjoyed by Jews in any country.
>
> I should be grateful if you would bring this Declaration to the knowledge of the Zionist Federation.

The Declaration was unreservedly endorsed by the other Allied powers—France, China, the United States.

Lord Balfour was undoubtedly sincere in his undertaking with the Zionists. "A man of extraordinary grace of mind and body," Beatrice Webb described him, "delighting in all that is beautiful and distinguished . . . aloof from all the greed and grime of common human nature."

Several Arab states, covering 1,184,000 square miles of territory, had been carved out of the defunct Turkish empire, and the victorious Allies had granted these states either immediate independence or the prospect of attaining it. Balfour expressed the hope that the Arabs would remember that fact, and would not grudge Palestine, a small notch in Arab territory, to the people who, for these hundreds of years, had been separated from it.

To all appearances the Zionist idea had triumphed. In Zionist eyes, at any rate, the formula adopted by the first Zionist Congress—a publicly-recognized, legally-secured home in Palestine—had become fact. The process of British interpretation and re-interpretation had not yet begun. In the United States enthusiasm ran high. Collections soared and membership mounted.

Henrietta Szold rejoiced, and hoped for a long tutelage under England—"as long as the Babylonian captivity." Her hope for seventy years of preparation was based on the belief that Britain intended to make the pact a reality; it showed also her feeling that a people with a two-thousand year gap in its political experience would not be ready to assume the full responsibilities of government without a long and careful training in statecraft.

Miss Szold's convictions on the value of an extended period of preparation were the result of her observations over a long period of years. The prosperous Jews of Baltimore had come under the lash because of their materialism. She had been offended by the lack of order in Zionist groups. One manifestation of this carelessness—

the bookkeeping records of the Federation of American Zionists—she had been called upon to clean up. "Augean stables" was her characterization of the condition. The Jewish populations of the midwest and southwest sections of the country, observed during propaganda tours in 1917 and 1918, elicited comments on their inefficiency and spiritual poverty: "The British Declaration passed over the heads of the Jews down here as an unseen airplane from one of the Texan aviation fields. They didn't know that something epoch-making had just happened. What an argument in favor of Zionism is such stolidity . . . The more they talk of the spiritual mission of the Jew in the Diaspora, the less spiritual are they Jewishly."

The problems she encountered on her arrival in Palestine in 1920 she found as multitudinous and as hard as its stones: "At the end of two weeks I was a wreck. I was ready to flee back to America; I wondered bitterly whether I had devoted twenty years of my life to an ideal that had turned out to be a will-o-the-wisp. For what is a Zionist who no longer believes in the Jewish people? In those first days after my arrival a voice kept shouting inside of myself: 'These are not your people. You have no part and parcel in them.' "

It was not only her difficulties with the personnel of the American Zionist Medical Unit that were responsible for Miss Szold's disappointment. "The education of the children is false," she noted, in 1921. "We are raising an arrogant, self-sufficient generation."

Unhappiness over the situation in Palestine was not relieved by contemplation of Zionism in America. She had no patience with a Zionism that expressed itself in floods of oratory when, to her mind, action was called for: "Action as against talk, and right action as against wrong." In a letter to the women's organization in America, the pessimism was transmuted into exhortation. Miss Szold explained that the Balfour Declaration, now ratified by the Allied Powers of San Remo, was an opportunity given beyond which the world could not go. The rest lay with the Jews: "Away with the propaganda of the word," she told them. "Nothing will avail but the propaganda of the deed."

Nevertheless her well-balanced nature did not permit her to succumb to despair. And there was one feature of Palestinian life which invariably lifted her spirits to good cheer and hope. In the *Kvutzah,* that form of collective settlement peculiar to the land, she found the answer to many problems. The fusion of communal responsibility with individual freedom; the happiness and satisfaction of the majority of the settlers; the constructive, vital nature of the work itself; the return of the Jews to the soil—all these were a source of joy. In spite of drawbacks—lack of system, lack of grace—the movement, as a whole, was in the nature of a miracle.

"The outstanding impression," Miss Szold wrote, "is the incessant striving of the people to create . . . Their interest in life is painful in its intensity. It glorifies—for them—every daily act, no matter how lowly, from dish-washing and cleaning to the vintage, and the discussion of an educational program . . . Within the four walls, as it were, of the Kvutzah, one does not feel the irritation of party strife, though the Kvutzah builders are the most determined and consistent of the partisans. They live their principles while talking them."

Miss Szold's enthusiastic acceptance of the way of life in the collectives, her recognition of the idealistic self-effacement of its proponents, did not blunt the edge of her intellectual understanding of the forces at play. "What I should like to know," she said, "is wherein the Russian system differs from the aspirations of our own Labor Party in Palestine. To me it seems there is no difference, except that the adherents to the system in Russia are in power, and carry out their theories to the last dot, while the Histadruth in Palestine receives its wherewithal from the bourgeois and must therefore, for the present at least, tolerate him."

Nor did she find herself in sympathy with a system which segregated the children in a community of their own. True, under conditions in the collectives, where adult members often lived in tents or in wooden barracks, the only means by which the children could be given healthful surroundings and good physical care was to build special quarters for them. But Henrietta's own memories of home and of the talk around the family table were so meaningful that she could not wholly reconcile herself to a system that separated parent and child. A child, she thought, should have the opportunity to store up family memories; without them its life could not be complete. It was many years before twentieth century psychology developed the same point of view.

It was not only the internal problems of the Jewish community that engaged Miss Szold's attention; she was also concerned with the relations between that community and the two other groups in the land—the Arabs and the British. In particular the relations of Arab and Jew colored her thinking so deeply that she measured the success or failure of Zionism by the degree of reconciliation between the two groups. This was for her the touchstone of the Zionist movement. Her awareness of the menace inherent in the situation persisted in spite of the assurances and reassurances of Zionist political leaders who either pooh-poohed the menace as non-existent or disregarded it as unimportant. Had not the political battle been won? Was not the triumph of the Jewish cause assured by the Balfour Declaration? Embodied in the Mandate? Signed and sealed by the League of Nations and by declarations of so-and-so-many governments of the world? Here was Palestine, tied up in a neat bundle and turned over to the Jews.

To Miss Szold the matter did not look quite so simple. The Passover season of 1920 had witnessed a serious outbreak of rioting on the part of the Arabs, as a result of which one hundred and eighty Jews had suffered loss of life, limb, and property. Waiting in Italy for her visa to Palestine, she met Mr. (later Sir) Herbert Samuel,* who was soon to be appointed the first High Commissioner for Palestine. From him she learned that the British military viewed the situation as serious. Later, on the crossing to Egypt, Dr. M. D. Eder, member of the Zionist Commission, told her that the British military was largely responsible for the state of affairs.

The findings of the British court-martial corroborated the statement made by Dr. Eder. The Jewish Self-Defense, it seemed, was on trial, rather than the attackers. Their arms, in their possession with the knowledge and consent of the military, had been used only in defense, but prison sentences were meted out to twenty-one of them. Vladimir Jabotinsky, their leader and organizer, received a term of fifteen years at hard labor. Miss Szold visited Jabotinsky in the Acre prison soon after her arrival in Palestine; she recognized his integrity and the cogency of his arguments, yet could not accept his militant approach.

Cruelty and intrigue continued their way in effective partnership. The keynote set in the "trial" of 1920 was followed by successive British courts. Of what avail the replacement of the military government of Palestine by a civil government when the head of policy remained the

* Served 1920-1925.

Foreign Office in London, when that policy was by no means a reflection of the convictions of this or that particular government in office—be it Conservative, Labor or Coalition—but was set by the traditions, self-perpetuating, of groups of careerist officials and carried out faithfully by flunky colonial appointees?

Miss Szold held the view that it was the British government employees who were mainly responsible for the agitation against Zionism. If these employees could not honestly accept the Balfour Declaration, it was their duty, she thought, to resign their posts. Instead they were instigating the Arabs and were instrumental in forming the Moslem-Christian Club, the organization which she suspected of planning the attack upon the Jews.

British complicity was made more and more clear by the acts of government officials. William B. Ziff, discussing this period in *The Rape of Palestine*, noted certain incidents: for example, Jabotinsky was held in the common lockup at the same time that the Arab agitators were accommodated in a pleasant room in the Governorate; audience was refused to Jewish notables while motor cars were placed at the disposal of the Arab leaders to bring them to an interview; Jews were searched for arms while Arabs passed unmolested.

A year later Henrietta Szold learned about rioting at close range: "It's no use waiting any longer . . . I thought I'd understand it and write to you about it, intelligently. But as the days go by, I understand it less and less. Only this I know—it is a very different thing from what it seems when you read a three-line cable in our papers at home about it."

She was having lunch in Tel Aviv when the outburst started in Jaffa, neighboring Arab town. Shots rang out. The reassurances by tablemates that they were merely warning shots being fired into the air failed to satisfy her, for she had felt an indescribable tenseness in the atmosphere all morning. The feeling of tenseness grew. She started out for the hospital, saw, on her way, that a war was on and, on reaching the hospital, found the victims: "Eighteen wounded were already inside, outside was a long line of stretchers with wounded and dead, in the yard the dead were lying, the operating room was jammed with wounded waiting to be bound up . . . We were there until night, and body after body was brought in. And in what a state! The little hospital looked like a shambles . . . And we had only the worst cases. Other hundreds were at the Gymnasium near by, at the Immigrants' Reception House, at the French Hospital in the city, and in private homes."

Far from being a spontaneous uprising, the massacre gave indications of being the result of carefully laid plans. Some Jews had ben warned by Arab friends to take measures for self-protection. At Petah Tikvah a small force of Jews and a contingent of Hindu soldiers, who happened to be on the road, stood against four thousand attackers. Four Jews died. On the bodies of eighty Arabs killed in that attack, gauze bandages and other material for binding wounds were found, leaving no doubt of premeditation on their part.

The first attacks were made in Jaffa, at the Reception House for Immigrants which had just received a boatload of newcomers. Thirty-eight of the new arrivals were hewn down by knives and revolvers wielded by members of the government gendarmerie, who had been sufficiently foresighted to pull off and conceal their identifying shields. Brought to trial, the assailants were set free because, as the defending Arab lawyers pointed out, there was no completely convincing evidence against any individual police officer. Jews who had used revolvers were convicted and sentenced to terms of imprisonment.

In the American Colony quarter of Jerusalem, where Miss Szold and her friend Sophia Berger lived, a quiet residential section inhabited by the elite of the Arab community, children of Arab neighbors waylaid Miss Szold on the road and pelted her with stones until one of the gentler neighbors interceded, and the stoning ceased.

The rioting continued for a week, breaking out first here, then there. By conservative estimates, ninety-five Jews and Arabs were killed, two hundred and thirty-eight wounded. In an address Sir Herbert Samuel asked his hearers not to be hasty in placing responsibility for the rioting, and yet himself pointed to the Bolsheviki as the inciters. In a personal explanation to Miss Szold, Sir Herbert stated that, had he not spoken and acted as he did, there would have been a massacre of every Jew in the country. Miss Szold commented that the statement was an acknowledgment of the fact that the Arabs were provided with arms and ammunition. She said further: "When some of us were told that timid words had been spoken in high quarters, because a general massacre of Jews was feared, our response was: Rather had we been massacred, than that one jot or tittle should be subtracted from the political victories our leaders had won."

The answer of the government to the Arab riots of 1921 was: 1- to stop immigration (1800 on their way from European ports were turned back); 2- to offer the Arabs a representative assembly, thereby enabling them to close the country to Jewish immigration; 3- to arrest Bolsheviki; 4- to arrest Jews who carried "concealed" weapons and defended themselves; 5- to set the assailants free for lack of convincing evidence; 6- to censor the Hebrew press. Thus, when the editor of a Jewish newspaper wrote: "The following are comments in the Arab press on the situation in Jaffa," the entire succeeding passage was deleted. It was legitimate, it seemed, for the Arab public to have access to information denied to the Jews.

All this under the administration of Herbert Samuel, greeted as the hope of his people, the modern Nehemiah coming, after two thousand years of his people's exile, to be the first Jewish ruler in modern Palestine! There had been an awesome quality in the welcome given Sir Herbert when he attended Sabbath services in the Old City synagogue, soon after his arrival. It was *Shabbat Nahamu* (the Sabbath of *Comfort ye*) so-called because those words begin the portion from the Prophets read in the synagogue that week. The streets along the road he was to follow were hung with gay rugs, with garlands of green, and with welcoming signs. "There was a suppressed excitement," wrote Miss Szold, "among the quiet throngs, largely women with babies in their arms, a feeling of expectancy was in the air, and on the steps of the synagogue a group of women with babies was sitting as though to wait for the gates to open to the Messiah."

Such was the mood that attended Sir Herbert's assumption of rule as the first High Commissioner appointed by the Mandate Government. There was never any question as to his personal uprightness, but colonialism was in the saddle and the misleadership of his official underlings, as well as the tone of the Colonial Office in London, made him fearful of the charge of bias in favor of the Jews. He was in Palestine as the representative of the Crown, and he leaned backward in order to avoid the suspicion of partiality toward those of his own race.

It was Sir Herbert who, after the trial in absentia of Haj Amin el Husseini (who in World War II made common cause with the Nazis) and his conviction of complicity in the riots of 1920, offered him full amnesty, recalled him from his refuge in Syria and rewarded him magnanimously with the office of Grand Mufti, thus making him religious head for life of the Moslem community, his salary payable by the Palestine government out of taxes collected from Moslem, Christian and Jew.

It was Sir Herbert who, at the King's Birthday celebration of June 3, 1922, pronounced the words, approved and signed by Winston Churchill, that tore the heart out of the Balfour Declaration—the words explaining that its terms "do not contemplate that Palestine as a whole should be converted into a Jewish National Home, but that such a Home should be founded in Palestine."

One more piece of politcal action must be recorded—the tearing off of Eastern Palestine and the creation of a new political entity, Transjordan, rule over which was given to Abdullah, brother of Feisal to whom Iraq had been assigned.

Sir Ronald Storrs, Governor of Jerusalem, credited with being Sir Herbert's evil genius, was described by Miss Szold as a dilettante idealist who from the cushioned comfort of his colonial office, his secure position in society, his assured career, expressed contempt for the Jews as rank materialists, for were they not such, he said, they would surely come crowding into Palestine, no matter how difficult the living conditions. It was the same Storrs who, during the period of mourning for the Jews who had died in the riots, arranged a series of festive parades and other events of esthetic interest. "The truth of the matter," said Miss Szold, "is that the Jew is not a 'native'; the Arab is. Kiplingesque!"

Among those who sat in high places there was one, Sir Wyndham Deedes of the understanding heart, Christian and scholar, who realized well what was going on and whither it tended. Helpless to remedy the situation, he chose to remove himself from the scene and return to England.

As for the Arabs, Miss Szold saw not the slightest evidence in these early 20's of any notion of the meaning of public spirit. There were no voluntary associations of any kind for public purposes—no schools, no hospitals, no libraries which amounted to anything. Only political aspirations were in evidence; their clubs, ostensibly social, served political ends only. At the same time schools and colleges conducted by Protestant missionary societies throughout the Middle East were stimulating anti-Jewish sentiment in Palestine and in neighboring Arab countries. "The Arabs, indeed, are most active at this tourist season," wrote Miss Szold. "They are distributing propaganda literature on the 'Zionist Aggression' among the American travelers. And the Christians are helping them efficiently. The Christians! There are some here who are reputed not to be missionaries."*

Miss Szold did not, however, spare her own people; unclouded by propaganda or self-deception, her mind could look upon its own as honestly as upon Briton or Arab. One charge she made was that the Jews coming into Palestine should have created economic opportunities for the Arab inhabitants as well as for the Jewish immigrants. Later she emphasized other factors as more important than the economic one. Baksheesh mentality, she said, blocked constructive thought on the Arab question: "And by that I do not mean actual baksheesh in clinking coin, but the

* The missionaries in Palestine were apparently making every effort to block Arab-Jewish understanding. For example, when an Infant Welfare Station was opened in the Old City of Jerusalem, located so as to serve both Arab and Jewish mothers, a missionary group opened a station in the Arab quarter, for the purpose of drawing the Arab women away from the Jewish station.

baksheesh involved in our thinking that, because our presence in Palestine helps them economically, their good will is purchased." The Arabs did not want the good the Jews were bringing them. Their answer was: "We will not develop so quickly, but we wish to develop in our own ways. We would be ourselves."

The other charge she made was that the taint of British imperialism lay over the Zionist undertaking. Yet she could not bring herself to renounce the dream of two thousand years. Palestine was empty. It could be made a land of immigration for the Jews without deprivation to the Arabs.

Jewish life in Palestine, in comparison with the materialism of British officialdom, Henrietta Szold stated, was compounded of materialism and idealism. She felt a glowing sense of triumph in the behavior of the Jews during the riots of November, 1921, (November 2, Balfour Delaration Day, and the spring festival season of the three religions were the two periods of the year most likely to produce rioting.) Better prepared against attack than in the previous year, the Jews defended themselves successfully, showing at the same time admirable restraint and refusing to indulge in vengeful counter-attack.

Pacifist though she was, Miss Szold came to the defense of bomb-throwing: "The trials of the offenders and supposed offenders are going on. The legal point is that bomb-throwing (on the part of the Jewish defenders) is not self-defense. My mind works twistedly on the business of bomb-throwing. I consider it the finest form of preparation for self-defense—the form least likely to lead to indulgence in assaults. Granted, as the government has demonstrated in Jerusalem in 1920 and in Jaffa in 1921, that it cannot protect the Jewish community, and the

Jews must stand for their own lives—then preparing a bomb is safer than constantly carrying firearms and concealed knives which may be plucked out of inside pockets on the slightest provocation. Bombs are not carried around; they are kept at strategic points."

The signing of the Mandate by the League of Nations in 1922 authorized Great Britain to act as mandatory power. The act did not raise Miss Szold's hopes—in spite of Article II, which assigned to Britain the "responsibility for placing the country under such political, administrative, and economic conditions as will secure the establishment of the Jewish national home;" in spite also of Article VI, which directed Britain to facilitate Jewish immigration under suitable conditions and to encourage "close settlement by Jews on the land, including State lands and waste lands not required for public purposes." The State lands mentioned in Article VI were formerly the property of the Turkish crown, and by the fortunes of war belonged to the victor. Though designated specifically by the League for close settlement by Jews, these lands were awarded to individual Arabs, and awarded in such lavish allotments that the owners were able to sell or to lease large tracts which they themselves could not cultivate.

Miss Szold saw in the Mandate not the ghost of a chance for the Jew—either to acquire political autonomy or to be trained for it. Not to have secured the international sanction of the League would have been a disaster; yet securing it brought no positive advantage. Whatever was to be done, the Jew alone would have to do. In the end he would win out, but the road to that end was to be measured in generations, not in years.

She clung to her hope of conciliation between Arab and Jew: "If our cause is wholly just and righteous, we are bound to find just and righteous and peaceful means of conciliation. We shall ally ourselves with the best of our Arab fellows, to cure what is diseased in us and in them. *Arukat bat-ammi* and also *Arukat ha-goyim*—the healing of my people and the healing of the nations."

10. *Jew, Arab, Briton—1929*

"The weight of the Arab question hangs on me"

IN SPITE of economic crisis and distress in the 1920's (see Chapter 7), the Jewish settlement made strides—the Jewish population rose to 150,000, an increase of nearly 100,000 over the pre-war population; agricultural settlements increased in number to one hundred; at the junction of the Jordan and the Jarmuk a light and power plant arose; tons of chemical fertilizer were brought out of the Dead Sea; periodicals and books poured from the presses; University buildings crowned the heights of Scopus. Lord Plumer retired from the post of High Commissioner and was succeeded by Sir John Chancellor.*

Into these orderly developments the events of the week of August 23, 1929, came crashing. Violence in some form was not wholly unexpected. What was not foreseen was its unspeakable savagery (so characterized by Sir John Chancellor), and the ineptness or malice of the government. The events followed a year of unease and preliminary rumblings centered principally around the West Wall, more commonly known as the Wailing Wall, sole relic of the ancient Herodian temple.

Briefly recapitulated, the situation and events were as follows. The inner face of the Wall is part of the enclosure

* Served 1928-31.

of the Dome of the Rock, popularly known as the Mosque of Omar. Its outer face fronts a pavement in the Moslem section of the Old City—a blind alley which, until this period, gave no access to the Mosque enclosure. From Roman times the Jewish community had the right of access to the pavement and Wall, and exercised its right constantly. On September 24, 1928, the religious exercises prescribed for the Day of Atonement were being held at the Wall. Shortly before the close of the service, Edward Keith-Roach, Commissioner for the Jerusalem District, appeared at the Wall, accompanied by police, and caused a screen to be forcibly removed. The screen, a portable one, had been placed in accordance with orthodox Jewish practice, to separate the sexes during prayer. Its forcible removal, during the most solemn ritual of the Jewish religious year, outraged the sensibilities of the Jewish community. The crassness of the act was the more in evidence by contrast with the care usually observed by the British not to offend the religious sensibilities of the peoples they governed.

The case of the British against the portable screen was that its use constituted a breach of the regulation that there were to be no changes in the existing set-up—a regulation which, they held, implied that no physical property should be brought in. Accordingly, the use of folding stools or removable benches had been forbidden to the congregation, even during the observance of the annual twenty-four-hour fast.

The months that followed the incident of the screen removal saw the regulation broken by the Moslems in a number of ways—by the breaking of a door through the wall at the end of the blind alley, thus giving access to the Mosque area via the West Wall pavement; by the instituting of a religious ceremony to the accompaniment of cymbals, kettles and drums, their use synchronized with the observance of Jewish services; by the use of the pavement as a regular passage along which donkeys were driven and sometimes encouraged to urinate on the stones of the Wall—sacred, said the Moslems, to them. Stones were thrown from the top of the Wall on the worshippers below. With the permanent changes devised by the Moslems, and the other entertaining and apparently legitimate activities initiated, the government authorities found it unnecessary to interfere.

Incident followed galling incident until August 17, when a teen-age Jewish boy, playing football, attempted to retrieve the ball which had fallen on the grounds of a Moslem home. In the course of the quarrel which followed, the boy was stabbed; he died three days later. A public funeral followed, during which the throng, though orderly, refused to be deflected from the route usually taken by funerals. The police charged the procession and many in the cortege were injured.

Among the Moslems rumors were spread that the Mosque had been bombed and Arabs killed. Emissaries were despatched to towns and villages, arousing the people and warning them to be ready for "the day," Friday, the twenty-third. On that day the Arabs flocked to Jerusalem in hordes, armed with sticks, clubs, pistols, knives. It was noticeable that there were no women in the incoming crowds. No attempts were made to disarm them except at one gate, and here the disarming was soon stopped by government order.

In the Mosque area and within the Mosque itself, inflammatory speech-making was the order of the day; the Grand Mufti addressed the crowds. From the Mosque the hordes poured out to the attack. Just outside Damascus Gate is the section known as the Georgian Quarter, inhabited by Oriental Jews who were completely untouched by political Zionism. The attackers swarmed up and over the gates, shouting their battle cry, "The government is with us." For hours the attack went on while, on the balconies of the Governorate across the road, British officials stood and looked on as at a spectacle.

On successive days attacks broke out in Hebron where students and teachers at the rabbinical seminaries, unarmed and unprotected, were butchered; and in Safed, and in small outlying communities to which the government had denied both the right of self-defense and the protection of soldiery and police.

In the course of the week one hundred and thirty-three Jews were killed and three hundred and thirty-nine wounded. Alarmed at the proportions which the unchecked butchery had reached, and at the focusing of world attention on Palestine, the government gave orders to shoot. No sooner was this done than the rioters were brought under control.

At the time these events were taking place in Palestine, the responsible Jewish leaders were attending the sessions of the Zionist Congress in Zurich. Sir John Chancellor, the High Commissioner, was on vacation in England. The British officials on the spot were Mr. Harry Luke, Acting High Commissioner, and Archer Cust, Secretary to the High Commissioner. Public opinion in America, not too well informed on the background, the issues, and the personalities, was misled by charges that the Jews had sought, even deliberately fomented, the disturbances for the sake of hypothetical advantages they might bring—the arousing of world Jewry, for example, would bring increased contributions to the Zionist cause. In his *Personal History*, Vincent Sheehan absolved the Grand Mufti of any responsibility for the attacks, and vouched for him as a mild-mannered, thoughtful gentleman, always open to reason, who had consistently used his influence on the side of peace.

Speaking before the Hadassah Convention in America later that year, Miss Szold pointed her finger directly at Great Britain: "The bitterness of the tragedy flows not from the artificially aroused fanaticism of unlettered assailants. We wondered, almost struck dumb, when our trust in the mature enlightenment of our sponsors was misplaced."

In England, the MacDonald government, Lord Passfield (Sidney Webb) its Secretary of State for Colonies, appointed commissions—the Shaw Commission, the Hope-Simpson Commission—to investigate and place responsibility for the crimes committed.

Admitting that "the outbreak in Jerusalem on the twenty-third of August was from the beginning an attack by Arabs on Jews for which no excuse in the form of earlier murders by Jews had been established," Sir Walter Shaw nevertheless exonerated his government. It had discharged, he said, to the best of its ability the difficult task of maintaining a neutral and impartial attitude between two peoples whose leaders had shown little capacity for compromise. As for the Jews, they were found guilty of being—Zionists!

Lord Snell, one of the members of the Commission, did not agree with the majority findings. He charged the Palestine government with encouraging the Arabs to believe that they had suffered a great wrong. "Progress in Palestine," he stated, "by which I mean the joint progress of the two peoples, is to be looked for not along the lines of political concession, but rather through social and economic reconstruction and the establishment of public security."

Later in the year the Hope-Simpson report carried on

the work of its predecessor, concentrating on a study of so-called landless Arabs displaced by Jewish immigrants. The study revealed that in the decade 1920-29, 664 families (688 according to Jewish Agency figures) had been displaced. With 400 families resettled (Jewish Agency figures) the total of displaced families numbered 288.*

The earlier British formula for restricting Jewish immigration had been laid down in 1922. Under that formula immigration was to depend on the "economic absorptive capacity" of the country. Since the factors determining economic absorptive capacity lent themselves to varying interpretations there were necessarily frequent differences of opinion between the Mandate Government and the Jewish community. Charges against the Jews of unreasonable demands were met with counter-charges that the Government's deliberate purpose was to stifle normal and healthy development.

Now the Passfield White Paper of 1930 introduced a measure which halted newcomers still more effectively; the more elastic yardstick was to be "political absorptive capacity." That is, the number of immigrants allowed was to be determined by the rises and falls of Arab temperature. The same White Paper provided for severe restrictions on land purchases by Jews.

The Permanent Mandates Commission of the League of Nations, by whose authority, supposedly, England was governing Palestine, expressed itself forcibly in support of the Jewish position: "The Jewish National Home, so far as it has been established, has in practice been the work of the Jewish organization. The Mandate seemed to offer other prospects to the Jews."

* In 1937 the Royal Commission commented that the shortage of land was due less to the amount of land acquired by Jews than to the increase in the Arab population.

Others, Lloyd George and Jan Smuts among them, raised their voices in denunciation. The London Times protested: "First the Jews are massacred in their National Home. The Inquiry Commission, instead of fixing the immediate responsibility, strays outside its terms of reference and blames the Mandate, the Jews, and every one but the murderers. Then the Government, instead of throwing the slovenly and biased report into the waste paper basket, proceeds to act on two of its recommendations about immigration and land, and finally proceeds to hang up the Mandate altogether until some one else has reported."

To Henrietta Szold the Passfield White Paper came with the force of a thunderclap: "We could not realize for a moment, even in our most pessimistic moods, that Britain —Britain, the lover of fair play, the lover of justice; at one time the protector of the persecuted Jew; in the days of Balfour, a nation that recognized for the first time in history the historic connection of the Jewish people with Palestine—we did not realize that Britain could so far forget herself as she has in her latest White Paper."

The Jewish Agency, which had just been organized at the Congress of 1929, was thrown into a turmoil. Dr. Chaim Weizmann, president of the Zionist Organization, whose credo was full collaboration with the Mandatory, now presented his resignation.

In the face of heavy denunciation on all sides and with the prospect of a test vote in Parliament on the issue, Ramsay MacDonald found it the better part of policy to backwater. Accordingly, on February 13, 1931, he laid before Parliament the paper known as the MacDonald Letter, in which he reaffirmed the Mandatory's "obligation to facilitate Jewish immigration and to encourage close settlement by the Jews on the land." The effect of the statement on practical policy in Palestine was nil.

Henrietta Szold's pacifist convictions now gave way before the facts, and her feeling that no reliance was to be placed on the Mandatory expressed itself in a forthright invitation to friends in the Haganah: "I cannot bear arms, but my home is open to anything you want to leave." "Anything" is to be understood as arms and ammunition. The circumstance of having no official ties at the moment to any Zionist body left her free to act in a purely personal capacity.

From another point also her new attitude was deviation. She had always held that close cooperation between Zionist officialdom and the Mandate Government was a prime necessity. Her conviction had been firm that, except for the care of the immigrants, every undertaking of a public character ought to be thrown on the shoulders of the Mandate Government: "Unless we make the government concern itself with us, it will never be our government in any sense of the word." The offer to allow arms to be brought into her home—the offer, by the way, was not accepted—was an expression of solidarity with her people. It did not indicate a change of view on the proper relations between governor and governed.

Still Henrietta Szold refused to look upon the Arab as enemy. Zionism, made a reality, meant the opportunity to translate Judaism into terms of practical life. Jewish law and Jewish ethics demanded a spiritual solution to the problems posed by Arab-Jewish relations in Palestine.

Self-examination went further. "Have we a share in the guilt?" she once asked an audience to consider. "Can one of us be at peace with himself so long as this appalling misunderstanding exists between us and our neighbors in Palestine? Are we content to be in Palestine at the point of a bayonet, whether the bayonet be carried by British soldiers or the Jewish Self-Defense? I hold that the matter of

Arab relations is our own peculiar responsibility, or at most the joint responsibility of Jews and Arabs. If we commit the unpardonable crime of looking down upon the Arabs as a lower race, then without a doubt the duty is all ours. The more civilized is responsible for the less civilized. But woe to us if we take this attitude. The Arabs are a race with a history. Nor are they all agitators or the dupes of agitators, nor are the educated members of the race all ambitious careerists. There are intelligent, wise and enlightened men among them who live in accordance with the behests of their Islamic or Christian faith. Nor are all the unlettered bloodthirsty fiends." She reminded her audience of acts of humanity performed by Arabs. She warned her hearers that Zionists must avoid claiming gratitude for the economic advantages the coming of the Jew had brought to the Arab, for the Arab no more than the Jew would sell his patrimony for a mess of pottage.

Because Jewish energies had had to be riveted on the revival of the Hebrew language, Jews had failed to learn the language of the Arabs. Because of concentration on the welding together of Jewish groups representing a score of psychological and national backgrounds, they had not cultivated social contacts with Arabs. Because the happy atmosphere had liberated their own creative powers, they had failed to explain themselves to the Christians, the Moslems, and to the whole world. She begged that, in Jewish education, every trace of chauvinism be removed, that the Arab language be taught seriously, that Arabic literature, history, customs, religion be made a part of every program of study.

Her political acumen—an acumen which many of her Zionist associates failed to recognize—enabled Miss Szold to see Palestine in the large frame of the Moslem world and of international world politics. Concerning one of the Moslem conferences she wrote that most of her friends were treating it lightly in the belief that it had no practical value for the Moslems, and implied no danger to Jewish development. She herself was of the opinion that the conference, even if it lacked immediate effectiveness, was important in being the first of a series, and dangerous in that it was spreading the poison of anti-Judaism to other Moslem countries.

To another correspondent she wrote, in 1931: "I am sure you will read between the lines that the weight of the Arab question hangs on me . . . To my mind it grows more menacing every day. I see the menace in proportion as I begin to understand the ways that are being taken by the nationalist movements in the Near and Middle East. India, Sir John Simon's *Report on India,* and Gandhi opened my eyes, Gertrude Bell added her mite, and I am now reading Dr. Hans Kohn's book on nationalism in the Orient. We Jews and our Zionist movement are but a speck of dust in these huge scales." Miss Szold was convinced that there was a mighty movement afoot, which neither France nor England would be able to control—a movement so mighty and compelling that it "will bring Great Britain herself to her knees."

11. *Jew, Arab, Briton—1936-39*

"The dust to which it may be ground
will be the living seed"

UNDER THE new regulations, the doors to Palestine, though not entirely shut, were left open just enough to allow a thin trickle to come in—1500 a month. But the pressures in Europe were strong and the stream of "illegals" that had begun in the twenties became too wide and deep to be held back: the stream from Europe was supplemented by that from Asiatic lands. The ironic situation arose in which the powers of the mighty British empire were brought to bear against the entry into Palestine of the one people whose home it had been declared—the home to which they were to come "as of right and not on sufferance."

Public opinion could not tolerate the Government's legalistic approach. On one occasion the High Commissioner summoned Rabbis Kook and Meir, the spiritual heads respectively of the Ashkenazic and Sephardic* communities, and lectured them on their duties as spiritual leaders to assist the Government in suppressing illegal practices, for did not Talmud and the prayer book enjoin respect for constituted authority? To which Rabbi Kook, a man of saintly character and of humble bearing, replied with dignity that he knew of no illegal immigration. He

* Ashkenazim—Jews from central and eastern Europe.
Sephardim—Jews whose ancestry was Spanish and Portuguese.

knew of sons returning to their mother's home: such return he refused to characterize as illegal.

"The business of illegal immigration," wrote Henrietta Szold, "with all the excitement it arouses among the Arabs, gets on one's nerves." Arabs from Transjordan and Syria came in illegally, over unguarded borders, in numbers greater than those of the Jews, some said. In their case Palestine's prosperity was the lure, not refuge from intolerable conditions; yet of the names in the long lists of deported which appeared in the press ninety-nine percent were Jewish.

The illegal immigration continued, and the Arab excitement with it. The three-cornered situation became further complicated by the growing complexities of world politics. On April 19, 1936, the situation came to a head. Thereafter, for three and a half years, until the coming of war in the fall of 1939, there was no let-up in the reign of violence and lawlessness, no period when life and property were free from attack. Terrorist Arab bands preyed on Jew and on fellow-Arab. Assassination was the answer to those Arabs of wealth and position who refused their tribute of funds to the terrorist bands. Some fled the country to escape murder.

Miss Szold charged the government with neutrality bordering on lies, with holding back evidence and facts: "Cold neutrality, especially with an undeveloped population like the Arabs, can work great mischief . . . Underground there is an effective, restrained, marvelously disciplined Self-Defense. All the staunch youth of the country is enrolled in it, to one's pride and one's regret. It's not the way—that is certain—of adjusting the Arab problem . . . Even the chauvinistic patriots do not deprecate peace and compromise talk."

The disturbances went on—knifing, shooting, beating.

Automobiles were wrecked by nails strewn by Arab schoolchildren under the tutelage of the Central Strike Committee; trees were uprooted by the thousand; grain in storehouses and in fields was destroyed by fire; factories were burned down. The High Commissioner, Sir Arthur Grenfell Wauchope,* expressed regret over murder, arson, destruction; and sympathy with the sufferers and the bereaved; but his words had a formal ring. He assured a delegation from the Jewish community that there would soon be quiet. The assurance had a sinister sound. "It might mean yielding to the Arab demands," said Miss Szold. "If that happens, we may as well crawl back into the German rat-holes and the Polish rabbit-warrens."

The questions which she and others asked remained unanswered: Why did the High Commisioner permit the Mufti to incite to violence—the Mufti, who was a government employee? Why did he allow dozens of government officials in all the departments to strike without filling their places? Why did he permit government departments to requisition the striking Arab taxi-drivers and their machines, paying them L2 a day, besides the salary of the drivers and the cost of the petrol? Why were Jewish passers-by held up by the police and searched for arms, while Arabs went along unmolested? Her mind gave the answer: 200,000,000 Moslems in India, Arabia, Egypt, Syria and Iraq—a powerful reason, particularly in the days of Italy's aggression in Ethiopia.

Excesses bred excesses and, among the youth especially, the feeling grew that time was not on the side of the Jews, that Jewry must not lean on the promises of governments, but must hack its own way, by whatever methods, to its own salvation. The hitherto unified and restrained defense corps lost members to the preachers of violent action. Miss

* Served 1931-38.

Szold commented with alarm on the "depth after depth of depraved, revolutionary tendencies among Jewish and Moslem youth." The only remedy she saw was incisive self-criticism and intensive work that would leave the teachers of youth no leisure for political agitation. But she feared that the youth could not be held in much longer. Her criticism was coupled with praise of their self-control: "They have been and are wonderful. At the funeral of the two nurses who were felled ruthlessly in the yard of the Jaffa government hospital . . . there were something like fifty thousand persons thronging the route to the cemetery in Tel Aviv, and there wasn't an untoward incident . . . To be sure we are not altogether innocent in this débacle. Some of us have been warning for years that the Arab relations question should be given first place on the Zionist program. Our 'patriots' wouldn't hear of it. No one can assert that consideration of the problem would have averted what is happening. But we should at least have done our duty. Certainly, it would still not have earned us the sympathy of the English officials here. They damn us if we do or if we don't."

On August 24, in the name of the organized Jewish women of the country, Miss Szold addressed a petition to the High Commissioner. She reminded him of the crimes committed during the four-month period, particularly those against the young—the attempt to set fire to the Babies' Home; the bombing of children at play in a schoolyard; the murder of a family of five in Safed, and the knifing to death of two young nurses at the moment of entering the hospital at Jaffa in order to minister to the sick, most of whom were Arabs.

She spoke of the discipline shown by the Jews, goaded though they were by wanton cruelties and smarting under the implication of cowardice; of the growing difficulty of controlling their impulse toward retaliation; of the attitude of the Government which made no distinction between acts of aggression and acts of self-defense.

Why have the murderers of the three score and ten Jews not been brought to trial? Why was not the train from which the bomb was hurled at the Tel Aviv railroad crossing halted and the passengers in the coach that harbored the assassin held for search and examination? Are we the only critics who think that the distortion of facts dished up daily to the public in the Arab press gives aid and comfort to the inciter who sits under cover, devising and directing attacks upon the life of man, beast, and tree? Is it possible that Government does not know the plotters and their whereabouts? Do not the immunities granted to provocateurs and their agents and executors account for the astounding phenomenon that until now no voice has been raised by either religious or secular spokesman among our Arab fellow-citizens, the possessors of a rich philosophical literature, to reprehend lawlessness, violence, murder, in the name of humanity and on the authority of the Koran, which is based on Hebrew Scriptures? . . .

Your Excellency expressed abhorrence at the brutalities recently committed, especially at the ruthless crime in the premises of the Government Hospital at Jaffa. Your words were unambiguous condemnation.

Our plea is for an equally unequivocal attitude and such determined action as results from an unequivocal attitude. We are confident that it is the only method of bringing about the subsidence of lawlessness and making room for calm consideration of the way of establishing harmonious cooperation between Jews and

> Arabs and between them and the Government, for the peaceful development of this tortured land.

The immunity granted to the agitators continued. It became more and more evident that it was the unalterable policy of the government to ignore the moderate faction among the Arabs, and to throw all the weight of its support to the extremists, thereby strengthening their intransigence.

Months later Miss Szold informed the Hadassah Convention that the shedding of blood had become a habit that had fixed itself alike upon Jew, Arab and Briton, that the Jew in Palestine was entangled in the mesh of hostile plotting. She spoke in pride of the Jewish community which pursued "its daily tasks, in the shops and fields, in the factories and the schoolrooms, watching at night, working by day, an antique picture reminiscent of the days of Nehemiah's rebuilding of the land. Nurses and social workers penetrated into every lane, bringing succor and aid, without thought of self. The drivers of public vehicles drove day after day along the ambushed roads, unafraid. Their coolness and resourcefulness in danger and their heroism in protecting the travellers entrusted to them, even while suffering from the injuries inflicted by the bullets of the waylaying bandits, have become proverbial in the land. The common man on the street, undistinguished and unnoticed, kept steadfastly to the straight and narrow path of duty, the duty of maintaining what exists and no less the duty of continuing to create, evolving and executing new plans and projects."

Miss Szold attempted to answer questions that she thought might be thrown at her if she were in America: "Can we go on with the Palestine adventure? Are we justified, in the face of recent events, in believing that Palestine will grant us what we hoped for—a life of security and normal development as a nation? I am not qualified to enter the field of legitimate political discussions and I have no desire to join the ever-growing company of journalistic politics-mongers who please themselves with a jumble of combinations and conjectures. On the other hand, the simplest mind understands that the political shocks to which the Jewish community in Palestine and its sympathizers beyond its confines have been exposed during the last few months are not without sinister implications. Its right to existence has been denied by its nearest neighbors, our Arab cousins, by means of declarations, strikes, arson, rifles, bullets, and bombs . . . Successive international developments have tended to shatter the belief . . . that Great Britain welcomes . . . even needs the presence of a normal Jewish community in Palestine, at the bow-knot of three continents, as her loyal ally in the consolidation of her empire in the Near and Middle East. Recent international relations and occurrences, shifting and changing with kaleidoscopic variety, seem to indicate that the Near and Middle East are populated by elements of greater importance to a world empire than the tiny Jewish group in Palestine backed by a widely scattered and distracted world Jewry."

Rarely did Miss Szold's moral stand achieve nobler expression than in the continuation of this message: "What I am about to say must be regarded as a subjective, personal utterance, the formulation of a feeling rather than an opinion. I venture to put it on paper, because it helped me to combat doubt and forge ahead with the work entrusted to my hands.

> "In these serious days, when Jewries in many countries are threatened with disintegration and the Jewry of Palestine in particular is under fire, I find myself penetrated by the belief that what has been built up

in Palestine constitutes a community different from any Jewish community in the world. I do not hold it to be a better community than any in the wide range of Diaspora groups. It is different: the difference is its indestructibility. The German Jewish community was deeply rooted in the German soil. It was intelligent and economically vigorous. In part it was consistently Jewish. Yet a political change has all but destroyed it. Even if the German political trend should be reversed, it cannot be restored unless entirely new foundations are laid. History has produced a second Spain. The Jewish community in Palestine may be harassed and impeded in its progress; it cannot be destroyed root and branch, as was Spanish Jewry, as German Jewry threatens to be. The political mill may grind it to fine dust. The very dust, I hold, will retain the character of the structure reared in Palestine by a fragment of the eternal people, borne on the shoulders of the vital elements in world Jewry. Its character springs from two indisputable facts: The Jew has an historic claim upon Palestine as Eretz Israel, and he has validated the claim by the volume and solidity of his achievements in the economic, the social, and the cultural field in Palestine in the course of less than twenty years. The nature of his achievement testifies to the fact that the genius of the Jewish people during the many centuries of dispersion was not estranged from the genius of the land of his national origin. The achievement is not an adaptation to another people, to a host culture. It is a revival of the land in the spirit demanded of the Jewish people by its legislators and prophetic leaders, during the centuries of its early history, in agriculture, in law, in social thinking, in civilization. The tang of Judaism and of Jewishness meets the senses of the student-observer of the Jewish development in Palestine. It will cling to whatever vestiges of the building will remain if catastrophes should be decreed. The dust to which it may be ground by untoward political events will be the living seed of another Phoenix-like structure."

The third claim of Jewry to Palestine—that based on the Balfour Declaration and its endorsement by the fifty-three member nations of the League—did not possess the quality of indestructibility that characterized the other two. It was the gift of outsiders, not the outflow of Jewish being and Jewish action. The third claim weakened as its supporters declined in power.

Miss Szold could not leave the subject without reverting to what she regarded as its central difficulty: "Nothing has been so depressing as the reflection that there is no plan for the regulation of Arab-Jewish relations after the subsidence of terrorism . . . We shall have to exist side by side with the Arab people of Palestine. The question therefore looms large: What will be the manner of Jew and Arab living together on the same territory? Will they, may they, continue to regard each other as antagonists? Will life in the central, indestructible community of Jews be compact of enmity and strife? . . . It is undeniable that centuries of occupation confer claims. That these claims have not, like ours, been vindicated in these latter days by notable achievements does not deprive them of their validity. The neglect of the land justifies our coming in and fructifying it . . . provided the older occupants are safeguarded. In justice to our past . . . we must seek and propose to our Arab neighbors the proper adjustment of claim to claim."

The continuing disturbances called for still another commission, this one distinguished from the others by its designation as Royal Commission. A group of the Empire's best minds, headed by Lord Robert Peel, heard and sifted evidence for months. Its voluminous report, including censure of the Palestine government for failure to maintain public security, closed with a recommendation for partitioning the country into Arab and Jewish zones.

The statement that stood out most glaringly to Miss Szold's mind was one made by the High Commissioner when he declared that the British government had done everything in its power for the previous seventeen years to bring Arabs and Jews together. "A monumental lie," she said. "I have been in Palestine all these seventeen years, and I can say with a clear conscience that the British government never attempted to do a solitary thing to bring about cooperation between the two races. Apparently *nothing* was in its power with respect to the reconciliation of Jews and Arabs." She went further: "We who have been close to the situation in Palestine can say that the British administration has deliberately thwarted every effort made by the Jews to find a method of conciliation between Jew and Arab. Here lies my attitude: we must have another five years of sympathetic trial to solve the Arab-Jewish problem. I believe there is a solution; and if we cannot find it, then I consider that Zionism has failed utterly."

On this point of British responsibility there was an interesting comment made by Dr. Judah L. Magnes in the summer of 1947 before the United Nations Special Committee on Palestine. He was struck, he said, by the frankness with which the government had said that it did not apply itself to bridge-building. That statement was in full accord with what he himself had observed during his twenty-five years' residence in Palestine. "It was always our conception that the Mandate was just for that purpose," he continued, "—to build a bridge between the two peoples. It would appear from this document . . . that the Mandatory was a sort of referee in a prize-ring where two combatants were fighting one another."

The proposal by the Royal Commission to partition Palestine into Jewish, Arab and British zones (the British to remain in control of Jerusalem and other holy places, and of the ports of Jaffa and Haifa) threw Zionist circles everywhere into seething debate, with Yes-men and No-men in vehement opposition to one another. To Miss Szold the proposed solution was an impossible one. She wrote to one correspondent:

"I wonder how you stand on the subject of the Royal Commission's report. Do you rejoice over the genuine hegemony of the Geulah (Redemption) as many of our best leaders do? Do you see great possibilities for us Jews in the tiny state allotted to us? Do you see even the promise of peace in the proposed solution? Here nobody, except those who believe the Jewish state granted us means redemption, is satisfied—neither Arab, nor Jew, nor British strategist. I certainly am not. How can one be with a Jewish state from which Jerusalem is excised? I believe firmly that our truly great achievements have been possible because we built on the foundation of sentiment, and Zionist sentiment is embodied now and forever in Jerusalem. The city is not the same monument to Jewish energy and creative action as Tel Aviv and Haifa. But it is Jerusalem, testimony and promise, the glory of the past and the greater spiritual glory of the future. Tel Aviv and Haifa are the present . . . They have no past and they will have a genuine future only as the satellites of Jerusalem, and the support of what Jerusalem stands for."

There were other grounds for her objection to the exclusion of Jerusalem from the Jewish sector of Palestine, grounds both ethical and practical: "It isn't only the absence of Jerusalem that I deplore and fear. I can see only an industrial, not an agricultural future in the territory, restricted as it is, allotted to us. That would mean that we should be deprived of the healthy return to the soil of which our people stand in need. I fear rapid filling up of every nook and cranny without the chance of slow amalgamation of varied populations. I fear above all the two irredenta—the Jewish and the Arab. I see no promise of less, only the threat of more friction and antagonism . . . If we have in our minds that, in spite of all, we shall overcome obstacles, and secure what has not been granted us, we are self-deluded possibly, surely we are not ethical. I don't like it."

For reasons unknown, she did not follow out her purpose to speak on the partition proposal before the Zionist Congress of 1937, but handwritten notes reveal that she had considered doing so. These notes disclose her fear that the prospect of statehood which the Royal Commission coupled with the plan for partition would tempt the Congress to accept partition: "What I see before us," she put down in her notes, "if we accept the Jewish state of the Royal Commission is . . . [that it] will compel us to keep the sword in our hands day after day, year after year."

One manifestation of the Jewish spirit in which Miss Szold most certainly took pride was the heroism and strength of purpose which found expression in the trying years of 1936-39 in the establishment of forty-nine points of settlement, many in isolated parts of the country. Between dawn and dusk of a single day, stockade and watchtower arose. Not one settlement was evacuated during the entire period, although many lives were lost in their defense. At Hanita alone, lonely in the hills on the Syrian border, ten lives paid the price of another settlement gained.

12. *Jew, Arab, Briton—Ihud*

"I reserve to myself the privilege of thinking, whether thought lead to agreement or the reverse"

MEANWHILE the Jewish policy of "restraint" had become the object of attack even within the ranks of Haganah (Self-Defense). Readers of Koestler's *Thieves in the Night* will remember the persuasiveness of the arguments there set forth on the side of direct attack and terrorist methods. *Irgun Zvai Leumi** (National Military Organization), an independent military body, headed by Menahem Begin, and an offshoot of Irgun, known as the Sternists† after the name of their leader, Abraham Stern, made inroads in the ranks of Haganah, but recruited most of their forces from the impressionable ranks of Oriental Jewry. Terrorism, aimed originally at government authorities, was being directed also against dissidents within the Zionist camp.

Writing in *The Palestine Review* of March, 1945, after Henrietta Szold's death, Elias M. Epstein, its editor, noted that Miss Szold had refrained from raising her voice publicly against the tendencies in the Jewish community of reckless partisanship, against the suppression of indi-

* In 1946 the Irgun bombed the King David Hotel; ninety-one lives were lost.

† In 1948, Count Folke Bernadotte, United Nations Mediator in Palestine, was assassinated by Sternists.

vidual freedom and the distortion of religion. Again and again she had asserted that she was not political-minded: in its narrow sense of chicane and treachery politics was certainly foreign to her nature. But in personal correspondence and among friends she poured out her thoughts and feelings—on domestic and international politics, on British colonial rule, Arab-Jewish relations, Zionist shortcomings, faulty educational policies.

As to why she chose not to give public expression to her ideas, the reason can probably be conjectured from hints found here and there in her correspondence. "I determined long ago to go ahead, no matter what messes the politicians brew," she wrote to an American friend. To give reality, so far as she could, to her dreams, was a compelling need of Henrietta Szold's nature. The impulse arising in the heart had to be translated by the mind into the slow, careful building up of structure after structure. Work—work in her chosen field—there lay her primary function. And a constant spur to her activity was her sense of the marching years and of the shortness of time left to her.

Concentration on practical work was the very core of Hadassah, the organization she had founded many years earlier. A piece of practical work was the platform on which all Zionist women could unite—whether their political views were right, left, or center. To her mind such an organization had no business adopting a political platform: "If such a thing as a Hadassah political platform were feasible, then it could not be true . . . that every individual member of Hadassah retains the right or the privilege during Congress elections to vote for any ticket. The setting up of a political platform tends to cancel such a right. If there is a Hadassah platform, one is not a good Hadassahite if she does not subscribe to it and stand upon it. But if there is no platform, a member is indeed free to express herself politically as she chooses, without in the least detracting from her Hadassah loyalty."

The two points made—that Hadassah should stick to practical work and steer clear of politics; that it should allow its members independence in political thought—were two sides of the same medal. At one point when the Juniors turned to her for advice on a question of loyalties, she warned them: "You do not owe to Junior Hadassah a stronger allegiance than your duty to yourself intellectually." Again she wrote: "Hadassah's practical ideal, the cornerstone of its foundation, has always evoked my loyalty, almost unquestioning. In the field of political thought and action I reserve to myself the privilege of thinking, whether thought leads to agreement or the reverse."

In the 1920's Miss Szold had joined a group calling itself *Brith Shalom* (Covenant of Peace), the avowed purpose of which was Arab-Jewish rapprochement. There were other adherents of collaboration between the two racial groups, notably HaShomer HaZair, left wing of the Labor Party, who struggled with the problem. Later she kept in close touch with a small American research group headed by Mrs. Rose Jacobs, the ultimate objective of which was Arab-Jewish understanding. Among the supporters of this group was the late Justice Louis D. Brandeis. In correspondence with Mrs. Jacobs, Miss Szold emphasized the necessity of organization discipline: no policy could be laid down, no action could be taken without endorsement by the responsible bodies of the Zionist Organization. At the same time she expressed her distrust of "the absolutists who blind themselves interminably to the uses of practical wisdom, who philosophize and dogmatize." Their approach she declared to be unstatesmanlike. Even the argument that the Arabs could afford to give up

Palestine because of their tremendous land areas lacked validity since it carried no weight with those "vested with the power of decision by public opinion or by public indifference"—that is, with the Arab effendi.

The choice, she said, lay between two instrumentalities—force and negotiation. "The first does not lie in our hands . . . It can be wielded only by those who will sit at the peace table, which thus would be turned into a table of incipient warfare. The second does lie in our hands, first with the Arabs themselves, secondly with others."

A tone of apology creeps into a letter to Dr. Magnes, written partly to explain her public silence and her loyalty to the official Zionist position. Her instinctive feelings, she said, rebelled against the official position, but she could not demonstrate the basis of her feeling—not in political experience, in profound knowledge of history, or in understanding of international relations. Her intellectual limitations were what made her a moral coward: "Suppose I were, with a word of mine, to destroy such good as may, after all, be tucked away in the folds of the negotiations I abhor and do not understand! . . . I resort to the responsibilities I have assumed, and silently hold that if I meet them to the best of my ability I am absolved."

But the time came when Henrietta Szold could no longer refrain from public speech. Here were her Youth Aliyah children in their thousands.* She had brought them into the country; they were her personal responsibility. In September, 1941, she broke silence with a plea "To the Yishuv," addressed both to the leaders of the community and to the people.

> These wards of our people, whose ties to parents and home we severed, were brought here by us to be

* See Chapters 13-17.

trained as citizens and builders of the new-old land . . . For their sake, for the sake of all our young men and women I would adjure the leaders and the led to remove partisan strife and violence from our midst. Intolerance bids fair to prevail . . . political scores are settled with bombs. License is tending to replace law among the people of the Law. Liberty of conscience and freedom of speech threaten to slip from our guardianship. Our hallowed ethical standards are in danger of declining. These are evil things, of which our camp must be cleansed . . . The Jew and his cause have persisted through the ages not by the might of the fist, not by the power of brute force, but by the spirit of divine law and love.

For many years Dr. Judah L. Magnes, Rector of the Hebrew University, had been advocating a proposal for what he called a "bi-national" state in Palestine. He defined such a form of government as one which would be neither a Jewish nor an Arab state. Without regard to majority and minority populations, the two groups would enjoy political parity, and neither would live in fear of domination by the other.

The plan was a hazardous one; its essential point was acceptance of the principle of compromise—a compromise abhorrent to all those whose single-minded goal was the creation of a Jewish state, and pointless, in addition, in that they saw no evidence on the other side of a will to compromise.

In August, 1942, under the leadership of Dr. Magnes, a small group of about one hundred people held a private meeting. It was a preliminary meeting, held for discussion purposes only, at which the program of a new organization

—Ihud (Union)—was to be considered, and plans laid for further discussion.

Before the new organization could hold its second meeting and complete the formulation of its program, a campaign began in the press, excoriating the organization—its founders, it program, its purposes and motives. In particular, criticism was directed again the group for its supposed acceptance of permanent minority status for the Jewish population—the subject of immigration had not yet come up at the first meeting—and for its supposed intention of inaugurating political action independently of the official Zionist bodies.

In the clamor raised against them, members of Ihud were attacked as anti-Zionists, and a proposal was made to read them out of the Zionist Organization. Said the late Professor I. J. Kligler, one of those present at the first meeting: "The fires of wrath were stoked diligently by Ben Gurion, and the sheep followed the shepherd."

The criticism did not budge Miss Szold one inch from her position. She continued to exercise the privilege of thinking. She charged the Palestine press with deliberate omissions and distortions, with baseless attacks upon the motives of the organizers and the purposes of the movement. She associated herself fully with Dr. Magnes in the pursuit of those purposes—the establishment of normal human relations between members of the two races through every possible channel of social intercourse, commercial contacts, public undertakings.

"Ihud establishes relations," she wrote, "and shapes them toward the end of forming public opinion. Ihud has no intention, even the remotest, since it has not the right, to appear and to act as the representative of the Jewish people. That right remains with our constituted authorities . . . This modest procedure was frustrated by the appearance of an unauthorized, misleading, and mischievous article in *Davar*. The other papers followed suit . . . [Since] when are discussion and investigation anathema among Jews and in Zionism? Have they become so in the year of grace 1943 when we hope for the victory of true democracy, Jewish and other, with freedom for the four freedoms to develop?"

Not long after the August meeting referred to above, Miss Szold had the unexpected opportunity of explaining her views to a visiting American who, but for his untimely death, might have become president of the United States. In a crowded day in Jerusalem, on his One World tour, Wendell Willkie had met and interviewed several representatives of Arabs and Jews. Miss Szold had been summoned with the others to meet him, but in deference to her years—she was approaching her eighty-second birthday—perhaps also in deference to her observance of the Sabbath since the late Friday afternoon hour would have made it impossible to return to her home before the Sabbath—Wendell Willkie took the trouble to call on her. They spoke of the problem of the persecuted Jew, a problem she had lived with for many years. "I cannot live comfortably in America while it is unsolved," she told him. "The Jews must have a national homeland. I am an ardent Zionist, but I do not believe that there is a necessary antagonism between the hopes of the Jews and the rights of the Arabs. I am urging my fellow-Jews here to do those simple things that break down the prejudices, the differences between people."

Baffled by the bitter charges he had listened to all day, by claims and counter-claims, Wendell Willkie doubted that Miss Szold's simple solution was a realistic one. "But as I sat there that late afternoon," he wrote, "with the sun shining through the windows, lighting up that intelligent, sensitive face, I, at least for the moment, wondered if she in her mature, selfless wisdom might not know more than all the ambitious politicians."

The attempt of Ihud to secure a fair hearing before the Zionist public failed before it could get started; its pleas for effective measures against terrorist groups fell on deaf ears. The terrorists continued their propaganda and their activities, particularly demoralizing to the young. Stink bombs and threats of violence were used against members of Ihud, all of whom had molded their lives according to the tenets of Zionism. Other dissidents were under attack. Workers who did not take orders from dominant unions were beaten up; printing presses which produced unpopular publications were wrecked; windows of cafés open on the Sabbath were smashed. Ihud continued in existence; but without its audience, the general public, its hope died aborning—the hope to make of Palestine a social laboratory where two peoples differing in religion, in social customs, in living standards, might attempt on the basis of their common humanity to solve the problems of their common homeland.

What Henrietta Szold's position would have been in the current situation, what it would be in any given situation cannot be surmised. No one has the right to speak for her. She is known to have said, in words that permit varying interpretations: "I do not wish to be quoted in my absence." Taken with absolute literalness the latter statement would nullify everything spoken and written by her. On the subject of Ihud, however, she stated, in words allowing of no "interpretation": "My relation to Dr. Magnes is the relation of the soldier to the officer." And the assertion may safely be made that at no time and for no reason would her political thinking have been determined by expediency. Her reverence for the ethical values in her religion, her understanding of the lessons of history, and the long range of her vision—all these would have forbidden her to seize an immediate political advantage at the possible sacrifice of remote, but perhaps more important values. The root of her fears lay not so much in external adversities as in internal spiritual inadequacies. Adversity, even disaster, she was prepared to face with courage: "Slow growth is the surest guarantee of success. For the perfect fruit we need a slow ripening—sunshine as well as rain; failure as well as success."

13. *Youth Aliyah**—*Organization*

"It deals with children—it is not child's play"

WITHIN the shadow that hovered over Berlin and over all the German land in 1932, young hearts palpitated and bewildered young minds wondered and feared. Recha Freier, rabbi's wife, sat in her study on the Alexanderplatz and faced the questioning of her youthful visitors. Where lay their road? To whom should they turn? She had no ready answer for the palefaced boys. In fitful rest, night after night, she pondered. Suddenly the inspired answer came—Palestine!

These young people, high school and university students, who had come to her, had long been active in Zionist circles, particularly as leaders of children's groups. Perhaps this was the moment to turn thinking into action, to offer, in place of bewilderment and despair, purpose and hope. Hitherto the immigration from Germany to Palestine had been on an individual basis. Was the idea of a *mass* movement of young people a feasible one? If feasible, how was it to be carried out? What agencies could be entrusted with its planning and execution? And what of Palestine itself? Would the community there welcome the

* Aliyah—literally a going-up or ascent; applied in Biblical times to the ascent to Jerusalem for the celebration of the religious festivals. In our own day the word is used to mean "immigration."

plan and be eager to prepare the way for these young ones?

The longer she considered the idea, the greater became its appeal. She discussed it with visitors from Palestine, and with German Jewish leaders. From many quarters came ridicule, with the derisive commentary, "Children's Crusade! Nonsense!" From other quarters, however, came serious consideration and encouragement. "Do it," said Enzo Sereni, one of Palestine's leaders, later to be martyred after parachuting behind Nazi lines; "It is a revolutionary idea. Do not allow anything to stand in your way."

In order to sample public opinion, Recha Freier spoke before an assembly of children who were about to complete their elementary schooling; she presented to them the idea of continuing their studies in Palestine. The next day her study swarmed with children and their parents who had come to "register" with her.

The idea had triumphed, but the means for executing it were not at hand, nor the agencies through which it must function. The older Zionists held aloof, skeptical of its value. Undaunted, the youth threw themselves enthusiastically into the task of organization. Under the name of Juedische Jugendhilfe (Jewish Youth Aid) they organized a central federation, the primary purpose of which was to collect funds for the transfer of adolescent boys and girls to Palestine. This central Jugendhilfe soon drew to itself two other bodies which had hitherto functioned independently—Ahavah (Love), an orphanage in Berlin, whose objective for many years had been transfer to Palestine, and Ben Shemen, a Children's Village long established in Palestine, but with its collecting agency in Europe. By the summer of 1933 these three bodies had coalesced into an Association for Child and Youth Immigration, the better to coordinate their propaganda, publicity, and fund-collecting activities.

Henrietta Szold's first response to the idea of youth immigration had not been favorable. In 1932 she was immersed in the social welfare problems of the Jewish community and plagued by lack of funds. When Mrs. Freier's emissary visited her, Miss Szold pointed to the needs of the Palestinian children and to the fact that there were no schools for masses of newcomers. But upon Hitler's seizure of power in April, 1933, such considerations became irrelevant. At that point the only questions to be considered were those of funds and organization.

Before the Nazi seizure of power—an event which to the world at large was merely a matter of internal German politics—and under the impetus given by Recha Freier, a small group of youths had made its way to Palestine, and had settled at the Children's Village of Ben Shemen. It was an experimental move which served to emphasize the necessity for careful planning in advance. Miss Szold's own time-table marked the official beginning of the movement as June, 1933, and the place as the Vale of Jezreel. Assembled at Ain Harod (Harod's Well), the representatives of the agricultural settlements of Jezreel, of all shades of social and political and religious opinion, voted to do their share in rescuing youth and making them a part of the Palestine community. Problems would have to be tackled—in particular those of housing and education. But the important thing was the will to take action: that the will was there was shown by the fact that not a single voice was raised in dissent.

The plan had been set in motion by the dynamism of one woman, Recha Freier. It now fell to another woman to shoulder the task of organization and execution. Now in her seventy-third year, vigorous and in full health, a lifetime of activity behind her, Miss Szold had been contemplating retirement. In the spring of 1933, together with her sister Bertha and a party of friends, she was making her last tour (so she thought) through the countryside of Palestine, revisiting its farms and villages, its hillsides and lakes. After this, she intended to return to America.

Fate decreed otherwise. Miss Szold remained in Palestine when it became apparent that the Hitler regime would bring large numbers of Jewish refugees into Palestine. Reluctantly she yielded to the persuasions of her colleagues, particularly of Dr. Arthur Ruppin, and to her own unrelenting sense of duty: "I could not but feel that I had acted rightly in staying here. I wish it had been 'right' to do the other thing. Here I am writing on Erev Rosh HaShanah* all alone. It is true I am writing in my room heavily fragrant with roses, lilies, and carnations sent to me by all sorts of people. But . . ."

The conviction that the Nazi terror would be of long duration may have accounted for her decision to remain in Palestine. "There is no hope," she wrote in 1933, "as many fondly believe, that the Nazi terror is, or can be made, a passing phenomenon. Hitler and his hordes have come to bide a while in this torn, agitated world of ours. It will be cause for gratitude if they do not ignite another world war."

The agency on which she agreed to serve was designed to prepare for the reception of the immigrants and their families. Youth immigration constituted one branch of the agency's work. It soon became apparent that Miss Szold would have to concentrate her attention on that branch. Her long experience in education and social welfare, the wisdom she had shown in the handling of organization

* Eve of the Jewish New Year.

problems, and her genius in human relationships made it inevitable that she should be chosen for the new task.

In November, 1933, Miss Szold visited Berlin, which was to be the organizing center for emigration. She found no understanding of Palestinian conditions, and much confused planning. "It deals with children—it is not child's play," she wrote. "I don't flatter myself that I straightened out the whole tangle, but I think the path is somewhat leveled." A parallel Youth Aliyah bureau was set up in Jerusalem. It was organized as a department of the Jewish Agency, but unlike the other Agency departments, the Youth Aliyah bureau was given complete autonomy. The unusual arrangement was an expression of confidence in Miss Szold's character and ability.

Miss Szold did not hurry the waiting young people to the waiting land. A pre-immigration program was established in Germany. Information about the candidates, their home and school backgrounds, and their religious affiliations was obtained through interviews and questionnaires. A careful physical check-up was made, with particular attention to eyes, teeth, heart and lungs. On the basis of this information a selection was made.

For a period of four to six weeks the successful candidates lived in camps in Germany, under conditions approximating as closely as possible the conditions they would meet in Palestine. This preparatory period served to test whether they were adaptable to new conditions, particularly to collective living, whether they were able to acquire a new language and new skills; whether they were, in general, physically ready for a drastic change in their mode of living. Those who passed the searching tests were accepted for immigration.

Legal contracts specified the obligations and responsibilities respectively of parents and of Youth Aliyah. In most cases the parents were able and willing to assume a large share of the expenses, including full equipment of clothing and shoes for the two-year training period in Palestine.

The process of selection underlined an idea inherent in Youth Aliyah from its start. It was not to be exclusively a philanthropic undertaking; its sole purpose was not the rescue of young people from a desperate situation. Implicit in the plan was the Zionist goal—the upbuilding of a nation, the accretion to its ranks of a sturdy stock, sound of body and of mind. The early formulators of the idea of Zionism had adopted, as an essential part of their philosophy, the necessity of transforming the urban Jew, estranged from the soil as a consequence of discriminating medieval laws, into a worker of the soil. To build Zion, he was to give up his commercial life, his academic ambitions, his middle-class undertakings of whatever nature, and learn to sow the seed and plant the tree, to dig ditches, drain swamps, irrigate fields, break stones, lay roads, put up buildings—in short, do all the back-breaking work necessary to a pioneer civilization. His children were to be brought up to follow in his footsteps. National regeneration demanded that he become, in the Biblical phrase, his own hewer of wood and drawer of water.

The practical difficulties in the situation, coupled with a progressive social philosophy, resulted in a unique form of settlement—an agricultural collective of a purely voluntary nature, financed, in its initial stages, out of Zionist funds. Various forms of collectives, more or less tentative and experimental, had been tried out in the early years of the century; they differed in detail, but followed the same general pattern. The major developments in these forms belonged to the years between the first and second world wars. By 1933 forty such communal groups were in existence, many of them in a flourishing state.

Henrietta Szold had always delighted in her visits to the Kvutzot, as these settlements were called. The sense of group responsibility was one with which she felt spiritual kinship, and the human material and spirit of joyous creation evoked her admiration. (See Chapter 5.) With the philosophy of work she was in full accord. That there were many Jewish peasants in the country was good, she believed. It was good that their number should be increased, for Palestine could be built up only upon a broad base of peasantry. She looked to the pioneer simplicity, even primitiveness of the set-up, as the means for strengthening and vitalizing the community. Her fourteen-year sojourn in the country had given her "ample opportunity to observe how Jewish creative powers have been stimulated by precisely those conditions . . . and how from the power to create emerges the joy of creation." The young people coming from the cities of Europe were to be trained on the land.

The Kibbutz (or Kvutzah) became the core of the Youth Aliyah system, although other forms supplemented it—the small-holders' type of settlement, the large children's villages of Ben Shemen, Ahavah, and Meir Shfeya, and many small institutions created from time to time as the need arose.

The joy Miss Szold took in the accomplishments of the cooperatives and in the spirit of the workers did not embrace all the details of living and working conditions. What she found most distasteful was the lack of order and system: "I love order. Disorder nauseates me. And they are systemless." In connection with the expected immigration of the early twenties she had been appalled by the same lack of system. "When I think of the coming immigration and look at our inadequate preparations for receiving it, I shudder!" There was to be no such lack of preparation for her boys and girls. The responsibility weighed on her heavily, so that at times she felt almost mastered by the impulse to flee from it. "The visualization of what is involved, physically and spiritually, in the transplantation," she wrote, "took away the breath, as it were, of my mind and soul."

The problems involved were indeed many and complicated. First and foremost housing had to be provided. Many of the adult workers in the farm colonies were still living in tents. The young wards of the nation might, as an emergency measure, be housed in barracks or tents, but that was acceptable only as a makeshift. The funds collected in Germany, and later throughout the world, were to be put to immediate use as loans to the settlements, to enable them to put up solidly-built structures, conforming to definite specifications. The buildings themselves, upon repayment of the loans, would become the property of the settlements, and the loans, reverting to Youth Aliyah, could be put to further productive use.

The problem of education, too, was boldly attacked. One of Miss Szold's reports touches on some of the difficulties:

> "Their [settlement] schools in all but a few places were developed only up to the fifth and sixth grades, to answer the needs of their own young children, while the Youth Aliyah demanded secondary school training. A new language [Hebrew] was to be taught . . . If, by happy chance, one or another knew the language, his exceptional attainment only added to the didactic difficulties; he required a class to himself. Nor was the Hebrew language the only new

province to be conquered; the average young Jew from Germany was a stranger in the whole of the Jewish spiritual domain . . . Nor does it tend to mitigate technical and psychologic difficulties that the groups are not homogeneous from the point of view of intellectual attainments and experience. Some candidates come to Palestine, having completed the elementary course and no more, some having had the beginnings of a secondary education, some having gone a little way along the paths of vocational training, and not a few having spent the two years since leaving the elementary school at loose ends, lacking discipline of any sort, unless it were such as is applied in the hard, remorseless school of sadistic cruelty."*

A definite age limit had to be set. Those not yet fifteen and a half were not equal to heavy physical work; at eighteen they were too mature to accept the role of school children and submit to an imposed regimen of study. The funds expected would not permit maintenance for a period longer than two years. Besides, the Government Immigration Department would not issue certificates to the Youth Aliyah for young men and women of working age. A certain ratio between the sexes had to be maintained—three boys to two girls—a ratio determined by Kibbutz necessities for work in kitchen, laundry and nurseries.

The plan of instruction covered a two-year period. Four hours of the day were devoted to study, the subjects being the Hebrew language and literature, Jewish history, the geography of Palestine, botany, physics and chemistry. Jewish peasantry in the process of development was to be an intelligent and informed peasantry. Another four hours were to be spent in the actual work of the farm—chicken

* During the years of Hitler's ascendancy the German system denied schooling and training of any sort to all young Jews.

run, cowshed, stable, vegetable and flower garden, plant nursery, kitchen, laundry. Evenings were given over to reading, discussion of group plans, choral singing, and other social and recreational pursuits. The program provided for trips through the country, in the company of leaders. With the Bible as guide book, they made acquaintance at first hand with the localities associated with their people's history, and with the new and striking developments of a dynamic community.

It was not only the two Jewish communities of Germany and of Palestine which were involved in making decisions. Not a step could be taken to bring in a single boy or girl without negotiations with the Mandate Government. Immigration certificates had to be applied for, made out specifically in the names of the prospective immigrants. Detailed and accurate data were required on each individual, and a guarantee given of full financial support for each young person over a period of two years. The preparation of the data, and the negotiations, verbal and written, consumed hours, days, and weeks of precious time. At one time, noting the normal difficulties she had to cope with, Miss Szold could not help adding: "When I have to deal with the delays and obstacles which the government delights in interposing, I rage and despair." She informed the Berlin office, when she pleaded for greater accuracy in statistics, that the government was imposing strictures and manifesting irritation at every departure from regular routine.

It would be less than fair, however, to leave the impression that there was constant friction between Henrietta Szold and the representatives of the Palestine government. She understood their problems, and her attitude toward them was always one of respect and courtesy. Her requests for immigration certificates never went beyond the limits of reasonableness. The government, on its side, appreciated her attitude, loved to conduct its negotiations through her, and on occasion, jumped regulations in order to meet her wishes.

Is there an undertone of triumph to be detected in Miss Szold's formally worded answer to the government's first inquiry for information about the refugee children from Germany?—how many children were deceased? How many had left the country? How many had left training in order to seek employment? She answered:

> "a) I am happy to state that not one of the young persons entrusted to our care has died.
>
> "b) Not one of these young people has left the country.
>
> "c) As far as is known to me, not one has left the place to which he was assigned for training in order to obtain employment."

14. *Youth Aliyah—Personal Responsibility*

"What the prophets promised—the return of the children to the fathers"

IN FEBRUARY of 1934 the first trainful of young settlers left Berlin. Parents, friends, relatives, envious members of the youth movement, crowded the train to bid them godspeed. As the train pulled out to the cry of "Shalom!" (Peace), from those left behind came the answer, "Tehezakna!" (Be of good courage).

On February 19th, the *Martha Washington* of the Lloyd Triestino Line discharged its passengers at the recently opened port of Haifa. Eighteen girls and twenty-five boys, with their leader, Hanoch Reinhold, destined for the settlement of Ain Harod (Harod's Well), spilled out on the docks with their suitcases, cellos, mandolins, bicycles and rucksacks. Grandparents, brothers, and aunts, vanguard of the German immigration, were on hand to greet them; courteous officials smoothed their passage through quarantine and customs. The gale and pelting rain did not dampen their high spirits and the festiveness of the occasion; they were ready to rejoice with the farmer at the blessed, life-bringing downpour. On the railway trip through the Emek next morning they knew and hailed the name of every station on the route, and burst into lusty singing of Palestinian folksongs.

The preparations for their induction into Kvutzah life had been carefully worked out. Rooms having been assigned, orders were given to proceed to the storerooms to take the necessary supplies of bed linens out of trunks and suitcases; to these storerooms they were conducted by a roundabout route, via incubators, workshops, and stables, so as to acquaint them with the lay of the land. The wooden barracks they were to occupy temporarily were well built, the flooring firm and closely laid, the walls protected against wet and mud. By the second day, with the ornaments brought from home hung on the walls, the rooms had acquired a home-like, cozy air.

"Religious poem" was Miss Szold's characterization of the welcome of the Ain Harod community to the newcomers—the solemnity and the joyousness of their attitude, the delicacy and tact they showed toward the youngsters. "I remained with them," wrote Miss Szold, "until the next day, saw them well bestowed, assured myself of the presence of screens, mosquito-nets, and sanitary installations. The Kvutzot were naturally not established as educational institutions, but they might have been if one were to judge by the way they make these fugitive youths at home, and prepare for their training."

The excitement and pleasure of the youth in their new homes knew no bounds. Miss Szold said that she would never forget how one group burst into song when from the bus they caught their first glimpse of Carmel and the lights of Haifa, or how delighted they were with the preparations that had been made for their well-being. They answered all questions joyfully, showing their close rapport with the spirit of Palestine. One boy, writing to his mother, told of the welcoming searchlights, the music, the flowers, the wonderful food. He went on:

It was hard for us to understand that they should rejoice over Jews coming to the Land. But here is *our* Land. They welcomed us: "Blessed are you in your coming, young wanderers." In spite of the crisis, they have received us with rejoicing . . . I spoke as the leader of the group. It was my first Hebrew speech, and before four hundred people! I told them of our joy in coming into a young Kibbutz amongst young men and women, and of our daily yearning to be with them: "Now we are here. Now all for which we were waiting so long is fulfilment. Yet it is still a dream for us. Now we shall begin our true life in the Land of Israel, in the land of building." And then the orchestra played again, and the choir sang, and we danced the hora again and again.*

These are articulate youngsters. One of them writes of the new language:

Today I am free to read. I go into the library and search the bookshelves. I take out one book after another to see which I like. I discover Dostoievsky's *The Brothers Karamazoff* in German; I am just about to take it when a Hebrew book next to it catches my eye. For a moment I hesitate: shall I take the Hebrew or the German book? But already I am leaving the library with the German book in my hand. At the door I stand still, I glance back at the bookshelves; and it seems as though the Hebrew book looks down on me with contempt. I go back to the room and something whispers in my ear: "Do take the German book; think how nice it will be to lie on the bed and read without any effort." At the same time I hear another voice: "Leave the German alone—

* From Norman Bentwich: "Jewish Youth Comes Home." Victor Gollancz, Ltd., London, 1944.

study, study! You cannot live in Eretz Israel if you do not understand and speak Hebrew." I imagine I am standing at the entrance of a deep cave which is barred by a huge stone. I know there are fabulous treasures inside, but only with great effort and hard work can the stone be removed and the treasures reached . . . I have made up my mind, and I take the Hebrew book. But I still stand before the bookcase.*

There are psychic changes–mysterious, disturbing, enlightening.

More and more the new grows strong, and the old remains only in the reading of German books; and it is overcast with a different light. Sometimes I feel that I am a new man with new clothes, and in a room with both new and old furniture, and I look on the old furniture with new eyes.*

Religious festivals and ceremonials take on new meaning:

In Germany at the feast our homes were decorated with green leaves, and the synagogue was filled with the scent of birch. But the meaning of this green was not clear to me . . . Now I understand! The orange harvest is over; the tomatoes begin to ripen; the garden is full of vegetables; soon we shall go out into the vineyards; the wheat is brought in for threshing; the flowers are in full bloom—this is the time to celebrate the Festival of the First Fruits! Now, too, I understand the meaning of our prayer: "We thank God for the good harvest."*

In the summer of 1935 Miss Szold reported to the Zionist Congress on the progress made since the inception

* From Norman Bentwich: "Jewish Youth Comes Home." Victor Gollancz, Ltd., London, 1944.

of the movement. Her appearance was greeted with a long ovation; when her address ended, the audience stood in acclaim, and showered roses upon her.

"Were I not close to seventy-five," she told them, "I would dare to make promises. I can only give expression to my hope that the little I did within my weak, human limitations will ripen into a blessing to my people and our movement . . . When I think how much self-respect our German sufferers have displayed, and that I was privileged to watch and to help to some extent, I must modestly say, 'The dear God has dealt well with me.' " She closed her address with a plea for the extension of child immigration: "That would be what the prophets promised—the return of the fathers to the children and the children to the fathers."

It was at this Congress that the German office of the Youth Aliyah surprised her with the announcement that a colony to be established by one of the graduate youth groups was to be called by her name. Established first in the Negev, the southern desert region of Palestine, Kfar Szold (Szold Village) was later removed to its present site in the north, almost under the shadow of Mount Hermon.

The Congress over, she proceeded to a Youth Aliyah conference in Amsterdam, thence to Berlin. Even though the Nuremberg laws had just been promulgated, the Jews of Berlin proceeded with their week's program of activities, during which they considered measures for training the young people who were awaiting transfer to Palestine. The name of Henrietta Szold had by then become a household word among the Jews of Germany. "They seized upon her appearance," said Mrs. Emma Ehrlich, who accompanied her, "as a sign that they were not alone, that the entire Jewish world was sharing their agony and standing behind them." She had expected to address a few parents and found six hundred facing her. She "spoke as if alone in the room with each parent, comforting them, telling them every particular of the new experience their children were going through. She knew the children by name, and their particular problems—the broken arm suffered by one, depression by another. The parents clutched at her with eyes and hands that would not let her go. She had almost to fight her way down the staircase, across the courtyard, into the waiting car."

She went to Berlin again, in the summer of 1937, to confer with the representatives of her organization and to report to the parents who had entrusted their children to her. "The middle-aged," she said, "have resigned themselves to their fate—they will rot in Germany. Their one cry is, 'Save the young.' " An eyewitness told of the crowded assembly, met to bid farewell to one hundred and twenty children, of "parents who in heartbreaking joyfulness sent their children away, of those who begged for the sorrowful privilege. Some came to look at Miss Szold, to show her photographs of their children in Palestine, and beg for personal news of each. What it did to Miss Szold we know who met her at the station at midnight, shivering and wan."

And so they came, first in their hundreds, then in thousands, first from Germany, later from Poland, Austria, Czechoslovakia, Rumania, Bulgaria, Greece, Turkey. Blown out by the noisome winds of their native lands, they found healing in the sunlight of Palestine, "in building and in being built," to use the phrase of their song. And always on the docks, awaiting her children, stood the gallant, aging figure of the "mother," of her who had said to her friend Jessie Sampter, seventeen years before: "Deep down in the bottom of my heart I have always held that I should have had children, many children."

She kept her fingers on the pulses of her thousands by various means. There was a system of regular reports—first on the child's entry and the initial stages of his adjustment, then on his educational progress, on the state of his health, on trips undertaken in groups and visits to friends or relatives. For any child who had been sick, a special form was sent and followed up weekly until the case was closed. So long as the European offices functioned, they were notified of developments in each case of illness. Whenever Youth Aliyah work called Miss Szold to Europe, reports on the sick followed her. Erich's health, she was informed, was at last showing improvement. Franz, in Yajur, had been struck down by infantile paralysis and had been transferred to Dr. B's clinic in Haifa. Wilhelm was now able to work as a gardener; the work agreed with him, he was putting on weight and the doctor was pleased with his progress.

One report made mention of the fact that the young people had decided, in their assembly, to forego the use of butter at supper on certain days, so as to contribute the amount saved for a public purpose—the planting of a forest as a memorial to five young men who had been shot down as they worked in the fields. At this the nutritionist in Miss Szold—or the mother?—took alarm. A letter was rushed off from the Youth Aliyah office to the settlement:

"We should like to know exactly what is meant by 'certain days'. How many? We should also like to know if the young people receive butter at other meals, or only for supper, and if not what they receive instead of butter. Another question. Is this the first occasion on which the youth have decided to forego a certain food in the interest of some scheme or other, and do your leaders intend to permit it frequently in the future?"

Personal visits were made in order to see that buildings

and equipment were kept in repair, and necessary improvements made. Were the showers in good working order and was there enough hot water? Had the broken screens been replaced, and the dust bins near the kitchen removed? Had the new toilets been completed? Were the mosquito nets in use and well tucked in? Would it not be a good plan to hang pictures in the classrooms? A lunch with the children assured her that the food was nourishing and the service pleasant, and the kitchen staff received a compliment for the neatness of its quarters.

"Religious poem," Miss Szold had called the manner of introduction of the youth to Kvutzah life. From first to last all who had any association with Youth Aliyah attested that the religious poem was largely of her making.

A friend, hearing that Miss Szold was on the dock at Haifa awaiting the arrival of a boat, hurried there to offer help. The small figure stood huddled in a coat, exposed to driving rain and wind. No expostulation could budge her. "My dear friend," she said, "suppose your son were on this incoming boat. Would you permit any kind of weather to prevent you from being on the dock to meet him?"

On a morning of frightful hamseen, when the desert wind had wilted the spirits and sapped the energy of all, one of the staff, finding her at her desk, as usual, at 8 A.M., protested. "What do you mean?" was the reply. "I feel like a young girl of seventy."

On another occasion, owing to a derailment, trains were not running. A telephone message notified Miss Szold that her trip to Haifa had become impossible, and that a member of the Youth Aliyah staff there would take her place on the docks. Miss Szold assented, but when the young man entered the port area, he was greeted by a slight, determined figure, which gave a soldier's salute. Miss Szold was on duty.

Each boy and girl became her personal responsibility; each ward, she insisted, was to be treated as though he or she were an only child; the thousandth as if he were the first: "When I rise from sleep, when sleep overcomes me, at all times this sense of responsibility penetrates and inundates me." In anger at the failure of a group leader to notify her of some change, she wrote: "I should like you to place yourselves in my position, responsible for every girl and boy in Youth Aliyah—to Government, to their parents, to the Jugendhilfe, and also to my conscience. I should like you to know that my request to be sent particulars does not spring from any bureaucracy, but is the foundation of our Movement." To another correspondent she stated that she had always felt that the movement must be a father and a mother, a real and delicate experience for each child entrusted to Youth Aliyah by the bitter destiny of the Jews.

The statement of principle was more than a manner of speech. It was found that one of her boys, blinded by a growth on the optic nerve, could not be treated in Palestine, but that there might be a chance for him if he could go to Paris or to America for an operation. The decision was taken to send him to America, even though the expenses would amount to L1000. Unfortunately the boy did not recover his sight, but he had been given every chance that the son of a wealthy man could have received.

Though every minute of her long day was devoted to work, no time was too precious when a child's need had to be met. One of two brothers had arrived in one group; the younger brother, Daniel, arrived some time later. Miss Szold took the boy with her from the port, up to the Jerusalem institution where the older brother was living. Not finding the headmaster in on her arrival, she waited for two hours in order to hand the child over personally to his care.

Entering one of the children's rooms on a tour of inspection, she saw a lad, in prayer shawl and phylacteries, at his devotions. After talking with him, she made arrangements to have him transferred to another settlement where the religious observance was in accord with the boy's own practice.

While self-government was the rule in the groups, certain regulations were of necessity laid down, and at times the wishes of the youth had to yield to authority. To Reuben and two others, who had appealed to her against the decision of their group leaders, Miss Szold wrote: "It is true that you have reached the age of eighteen, a responsible age, but you should understand, too, that both we and your *madrich* (leader) have acquired much experience in the course of the years, and your interests concern us just as much as they concern you. You would be wise to avail yourselves of the opportunity of receiving good advice as long as you are able to."

One of the most interesting cases in which she had a hand was that of Avigdor Dlugacz. Dlugacz was a boy of fifteen when he arrived in Palestine after years of living in concentration camps. A worker from the office, visiting the youth group at Maale HaHamisha (Hill of the Five), saw him at work on sketches of camp scenes, done from memory. Impressed by the vigor of the untaught boy's drawing, she suggested that he send an album of his sketches to Miss Szold. In a short time a letter to the group leader arrived, asking that the boy be sent to her. Frightened and excited, the boy arrived at the hospital where Miss Szold's last illness was confining her, expecting to be faced by a formidable personage. He was ushered into the presence of an old lady who welcomed him in a weak voice and asked him to sit down. Drawing the album out of her desk, she questioned him closely. Were these his own sketches, or had he copied some pictures he had seen? Failing to grasp the purport of her questions, Avigdor believed her to be doubtful of the facts of life in concentration camps as he had known and sketched them. He proceeded to recount gruesome details in order to convince her of the truth of his experiences. He pointed to his sketch of the wagon of the dead in which he had seen his own father's body removed. Convinced that the boy had himself witnessed the grim scenes, and that his sketches were original, she told him he would be given the opportunity for study in art. Thereafter Avigdor spent part of the day studying art at the Bezalel Institute in Jerusalem, the other part doing his share of work at the Kvutza of Maale HaHamisha. He is ambitious to pursue his studies, and dreams of specializing in murals; he hopes to return thanks to the land which gave him refuge by painting murals on the walls of the collectives. Not the least of his pride is that the choice fell on him, in the pilgrimage to Miss Szold's grave on the anniversary of her death, to recite the Kaddish, traditional prayer of mourners. In that recital his is the voice of all Youth Aliyah.

Like any mother who delights in recounting the special joys of the household, Miss Szold recounted, in glee and excitement, the story of one such joy. On the *Darien*, refugee boat whose eight hundred passengers had reached the shores of Palestine after five months by road and water, were sixty children. In accordance with government practice, all passengers were sent to the internment camp at Athlit. The children's release could not be secured. To keep them occupied and to accustom them to discipline, a teacher was sent to the camp. Although text books, reading matter, sports equipment and materials for light work were provided, the camp was no place for adolescents. She determined on an appeal to the High Commissioner for a personal interview; she was resolved to describe to him the conditions in Athlit, as they affected young children—citizens of the future, to whatever country they might find their way. A coolly-worded response arrived from the Secretariat, suggesting that the interview be deferred until a more opportune time because "in view of the question of policy involved, it is unlikely that his Excellency will be able to acquaint you with any decision in the immediate future." Nevertheless, permission was given for the interview, if she insisted, in five days' time.

When she arrived at the High Commissioner's residence, she was notified that the children were to be freed. It was mid-morning; on the following evening, the Passover Seder, festival of freedom, was to be celebrated. Miss Szold mentioned this fact and asked his Excellency whether the children could be released in time to celebrate the Passover. Permission was granted, provided that all formalities were complied with.

Miss Szold and Hans Beyth, her right hand, proceeded at once to the Secretariat, received detailed instructions and secured a permit from the police for Beyth to enter the camp that day. At one o'clock, armed with a list of those to be released, Beyth went to the camp to secure the consent of the parents. Overjoyed, the parents requested that every effort be made to remove the children at once. At midnight Hans was back in Jerusalem, reporting to Miss Szold on the details of the discussions with the camp authorities, the Youth Aliyah representatives, and the parents. The next morning copies of the list were presented to the Secretariat and to the Police Departments for the necessary endorsements. A new permit to enter the camp that day had to be secured. Finally, all formalities complied with, Hans reentered the camp at 3.15, and piled the children into the autobus that had been engaged that morning for the purpose. The children had their Seder that night. Not so Hans Beyth, who returned to his home rejoicing, but too exhausted to do anything but tumble into bed.

"There is the whole story," Miss Szold wrote. "What I want you to read into it is the courtesy of all government offices and personages, and our fervent hope that we may be able to continue without intermission to salvage refugees."

On another occasion when after a long, bitter wait one hundred certificates were received from the government—certificates which meant the salvaging of one hundred young lives—she could not contain her joy: "I felt as heady as though I had been indulging in champagne. Literally I found myself unable to settle down to work."

An associate tells that when Miss Szold first consented to head the Youth Aliyah she stated that she would start the ball rolling, then let others take over. Later she announced, in turn, that she would wait for the thousandth child, then for the five thousandth, and for the ten thousandth. Her great regret when the numbers rose above the two thousand mark was the impossibility of continuing in close, personal touch with each and every one of the children. Yet each group, each settlement, felt itself her special darling, the object of her special attention. Proudly each one tells the visitor, "But, you know, Miss Szold was especially interested in us."

During the tenth anniversary tour of Youth Aliyah settlements, arranged for the benefit of the press, a change in program necessitated a postponement of one of the visits. Alonim (Oaks), first of the "graduate" settlements, scheduled for the final evening visit of the crowded first day, could not be reached. Word of the change was telephoned

—the visitors would come next morning. But unannounced, Miss Szold left the party and arrived that night, excited and eager. "It's good the others didn't know how my heart was beating. I understand it. Maybe there's a difference between the first-born and the others, the later ones." The days of that tour of inspection were joyous days for her.

For the Youth Aliyah groups all her visits of inspection were holidays. On one occasion silence greeted her at the gate—not a welcoming voice or hand. Suddenly from the trees flanking the gate the fledglings of the village dropped to the ground, chirping and twittering merry greetings to their beloved friend.

"There is nothing new in my chronicle," she writes to her sister, and proceeds to enumerate the day's items: "Help requested for a graduate of five years' standing, who joined the army, was left paralyzed in her lower limbs by an automobile accident; a child with heart trouble among the Teheran group, who must be doctored and given special care forever; a graduate, particularly talented, wants a stipend to pursue higher studies; a woman from Bucharest who describes the sufferings of 8000 children deported from the Bukowina and Bessarabia to Transdniestria—3000 dead, 4000 gathered by women's organizations in Bucharest by underground methods, sheltered in an orphanage, 1000 still wandering, famished, naked, sick; the representation of the Yemenite communities who insist on 'butting in' at Meir Shfeya where we are caring for a group of Yemenite children; young Polish parents whose baby sickened, on their flight from Warsaw, with pneumonia, caught diphtheria in a village hospital, went blind from undernourishment while at the hospital, could not be circumcised, and (as they stated) is being refused admission to the Institute for the Blind on account of the failure to be circumcised, while the physician forbids the operation; in between, telephone calls: the children to be transferred from Mikveh Israel to S'deh Jacob refuse to go; and cables: Turkey demands two hundred fifty more youth certificates; dictating letters: to Government requesting the despatch of six certificates to Nairobi where children of Jewish parents left behind in Russia are in a Polish encampment, and two dozen others. Still it is true; there is nothing new in my chronicle."

And to her friend Dr. Friedenwald: "There is not a vestige of self-esteem in my agreement with your judgment that the Youth Aliyah is the best thing we Jews are doing. I have never been concerned with anything in the way of public work which as impressively as Youth Aliyah made me feel that I am an instrument in the hands of a Higher Power; hence, no self-esteem. As for its value in all respects, one has but to look at the brawny young men and the spirited young women the movement develops to be impressed with the human and citizenship material shaping itself to the uses of a New Palestine."

15. *Youth Aliyah—Education*

"into the past for inspiration and into the future for action"

INTEGRATION into the life of Palestine, as noted earlier, meant not only acquiring the habit of work on the land. It meant as well becoming acquainted with a people—its character, its history, its aspirations. Special material, simply presented, had to be prepared in Hebrew for those just beginning to grapple with the complexities of a strange tongue.

In her introduction to the special series of pedagogic material, Miss Szold recommended that both the selection of material and the method of instruction be free from routine: "A mere story of successive happenings would be a rope of iron chaining the young to the spot on which they stand, while what they need and in these days crave is a power propelling them into the past for inspiration and into the future for action."

To the young students themselves she gave warning not to reject the spiritual values of their past, the values created by Goethe, Lessing and Schiller, but to continue their reading of German literature at least until they had acquired enough Hebrew to take its place. And she exclaimed in amazement and delight at the rapidity and ease with which the children learned to express themselves in the new and difficult tongue.

While she approved, in general, of training the children for rural life, Miss Szold chafed at the rigidity of the educational pattern. She could not reconcile herself to the Procrustean bed which forced every girl and boy into the same mold. The fundamental principle of farm training must be held to, but the application of the principle should not preclude an intelligent and merciful consideration of inclination and previous training. It took time, however, to develop schools for giving boys the vocational training some of them craved. Time—and money, which came, never in fully adequate amounts but in good enough supply to satisfy at least part of the need for vocational and even professional training.

Serious psychological problems sometimes raised ugly heads. One youth, unable to adapt himself to group living, could affect adversely the tone and spirit of the entire group. To be sure, the boy unable or unwilling to perform physical work, to forego the desire for an academic or professional career, would be rejected by the group itself; so also the "malingerer, the truant from studies, the meddler who abuses the fellowship and violates the decencies of communal living." That might dispose of the problem so far as the group was concerned. Not so for the Youth Aliyah organization whose problem he remained.

Occasionally there came to Palestine a romantic young girl or boy who looked upon the novel experience as a lark, and failed at first to face the realities of the situation squarely. Among the leaders, too, some were affected by this romanticism. A young woman from Germany, having completed her medical training, had refused to take her final examinations; she was determined to lead a life of physical labor in Palestine. After talking the matter over with Miss Szold, she was persuaded to give up that plan. She returned to Germany, in time to take her examinations, then went again to Palestine and took up there the practice of medicine in which she is now happily engaged.

Parents and relatives were sometimes a distracting influence, desiring for one reason or another to break in on a young relative's educational program. For the six or seven desertions out of the first seven hundred immigrants, the responsibility lay with the parents. Miss Szold refused to lend an ear to sentimental appeals. To one man who complained that his young son was physically and spiritually broken, presenting the lad's letter in proof, she replied callously that she had received letters of that kind in such number that she was prepared to write one which might pass for Karl's own.

In her guardianship of the young people Miss Szold enjoyed the assistance of a loyal and devoted staff of workers, both in the field and in her office—"the most efficient, devoted help that mortal was ever blessed with." At her right hand stood her deputy, Hans Beyth. In his early twenties Hans had spent a vacation of a few months in Palestine. He had returned to Germany a Zionist, and had thereafter given much of his leisure to promoting the idea of Zionism, particularly among the youth. Late in 1934, the German office of Youth Aliyah called on him for service in Palestine. Henrietta Szold, they told him, needed some one who understood finance. Would he go? To Palestine, yes. To the office of Youth Aliyah, no. He had been trained in banking, and he wished to continue in a business for which he was qualified. To switch to social service, in which he was merely an amateur, was unthinkable. However, he agreed to see Miss Szold when he arrived in Palestine.

These negotiations had been carried on without consultation with Miss Szold. She was aghast on being told that an unknown gentleman had been invited to join her office staff. But in their first interview, each was completely won by the other's charm and the matter was quickly decided. Hans remained, first in charge of financial matters, later as deputy for Miss Szold in organization and in field work.*

At her other hand stood Mrs. Emma Gomborow Ehrlich, personal secretary, friend, younger sister, daughter. Coming to Miss Szold at the age of fourteen, taught by her, trained by her, she gave in return a lifetime of disinterested service, and took the place in Miss Szold's heart of the child she craved and had never borne. "All I can say," Miss Szold had written her as early as 1923, "is that I cannot conceive of myself doing without you."

After Miss Szold's death Dr. Magnes wrote to Mrs. Ehrlich: "That great woman, who was surrounded by the affection of thousands, was nevertheless very lonely, and it was you who brought the comfort and companionship she craved. It was not given to everyone, as it was given to me, to see the gentleness and patience and companionship of your presence all these last months. This meant more to her than even you know. Your service to her was unique in every way—without it I cannot picture what these last months would have been."

Miss Szold depended to a great extent on the workers in the field. The *Madrichim,* combining the functions of teacher and big brother (or sister), were, she said, her teachers. Her confidence was not misplaced. Any one seeing these men and women in company with their groups cannot help being impressed with their moral and intellectual quality, and their warm-hearted personalities.

* That interview sealed Hans's fate in another way. On December 26, 1947, a mission to the harbor to receive a contingent of newcomers was no longer a routine trip. It was taken at mortal risk. On the return trip the convoy in which Hans was riding was ambushed by Arab snipers. As the only one in the bus licensed to bear arms, he rose to answer the attack, and fell, riddled by Arab bullets.

There is a musician at Ben Shemen who, in spite of having lost an arm, plays his instrument in masterly fashion and conducts his choruses and orchestras. The room of another is a library for art lovers to revel in. In another children's village lives a gentle couple who treasure within the walls of their one room the few mementos they brought with them of an earlier, more gracious day. The family portraits bespeak a heritage which goes back to the Germany of the 1700's. Their future is rooted in this old-new land by the lives of four farmer sons and the birth of grandchildren.

One of the most widely known of all the *Madrichim* is the shepherd Mattatyahu (Mattathias), turned from a keeper of sheep to a keeper of souls. His songs of nature are sung through the length and breadth of the land. He dedicates his gifts to his young charges; for them he writes a play portraying sheep-shearing as carried on in Biblical times. His are both text and music; he trains the actors, and teaches them to play the pipe and to sing the songs.

Into the consecrated hands of these leaders Henrietta Szold delivered her charges. She gave of her strength and her courage, and received it back a hundred-fold. There were times of protracted waiting, in deferred hope, for the arrival of child refugees. At one such time she addressed the leaders:

> I am compelled to turn to you because in addressing you I hope to renew my own courage and faith . . . For the moral strength to persist unflinchingly I turn to you whose source of strength is your daily contact with the youth which is in your charge.
>
> I envy you. Your duty lies defined before you. The darker the outlook, the more clearly you see your task—to teach, to train, to influence, to open up vistas

into the past and into the future. It is for you to heal wounds inflicted by malign cruelty, to replace the wrenched ties that bound a generation of children to fathers and mothers scattered to the farthest corners of the earth, to restore confidence in men and in their works, to evoke powers and direct them to worthy ends, to set up ideals in conformity with the secular achievements of human and of Jewish endeavor, to strengthen moral fiber, to encourage aspiration and direct it into channels of action towards culture and peace . . .

When I summon before my mind's eye the picture of a regiment of several hundred *Madrichim* intent upon such task, my courage and my faith revive, and I am assured that our hope cannot fail.

One of the leaders' most vivid memories of Henrietta Szold is associated with the tragic news of the fall of Paris in 1940. The news came when they were gathered for one of their periodical seminars; it reduced all of them, the young and the not-so-young, to a state of complete dejection. Then Henrietta Szold spoke out of the fullness of her seventy-nine years—spoke of the fall of Paris in 1871, which she remembered; spoke of the Commune that followed; reminded them of the situation during the First World War when Paris, in desperate straits, with the enemy almost at her gates, was miraculously saved. Now, too, she assured them, there was no question as to the final outcome of the war: Paris would again be French.

There was close rapport between the Youth Aliyah Bureau and the settlements. The relationship stood them all in good stead. Once word arrived of forty children coming from Europe. The plan for their placement proved unacceptable to the government. A desperate search got under way for another settlement—one which would meet government approval and which could undertake the care of forty children. The search was the more desperate in that, after twenty-four hours, the immigration certificates for these particular children would expire. If a place for them could not be found within that period, the children would be denied admittance to the country; nor could the lapsed certificates be turned to use for other children.

The government had indicated that the colony of Beer Tuvia would be acceptable. The difficulty lay in communicating with Beer Tuvia. There was no telephonic connection, and the drive down and back could not be made within the allotted time. A frantic telephone message went to Givat Brenner. Could a messenger on horseback get down to Beer Tuvia and back in time? Impossible, but there would be communication set up with Beer Tuvia.

That night light signals flashed from tower on the hill to tower in the plain.

"Will you take a group of German children?"

"Yes, yes."

"Can you provide living quarters for them?"

"Yes, yes."

"Will you take forty?"

"No—sixty."

From time to time there came to Miss Szold's desk expressions of concern from relatives of the youngsters or from donors to Youth Aliyah—concern that the collectives did not provide the right environment for bringing up young people. With such attitudes the Victorian lady had no sympathy. To one inquirer she wrote that in dealing with the sixty problem cases that had arisen among the fourteen hundred children under her care, her stay and support had been the Youth Aliyah committees in the Kvutzot: "They observe the cases, they analyze them, they report upon them to me, they summon me to observe the problematic cases, they never merely push the cases onto my shoulders. . . . Consideration of some cases has extended over many months . . . The sound and sage advice of the committees has enabled me to rescue a number of boys and girls who were in danger of yielding to the temptations incidental to adolescence. I can say that the Kvutzah has taught me much.

"I do not mean to imply that the Kvutzah system makes saints of its members. They remain human beings with faults and foibles. I do want to convey to you that they are alive to their responsibility toward the young people they have gathered in, and that they are equally alive to the nature of the dangers that beset them. The Kvutzot are built up on a new social system that not all of us can accept, but from what is called the 'moral' point of view, I should be willing to entrust a child of mine to their ministrations."

16. *Youth Aliyah—Teheran*

"The head and front of my offending"

THE CRASH of war broke into the carefully organized functioning of Youth Aliyah. Children in European training camps and in temporary homes—in Holland, Luxembourg, Denmark, France, England—were waiting for the word of release. Many in Central Europe, who had completed their training and were in possession of the coveted certificates of entry into Palestine, were caught by the advancing Nazi horror. A few managed to slip through. Others, waiting through slow months, ruefully added to their camp songs: "It's a long, long way to a permit." For great numbers it was road's end.

In Palestine, meanwhile, Youth Aliyah graduates had completed their prescribed training and were joining adult groups or preparing to organize new settlements. The settlements they were leaving pleaded and clamored for new groups of young people to fill the empty living quarters. Why should not these homes be put to immediate use, opened to some of the young Palestinians of whose need Miss Szold was so well aware? Permission was secured from Hadassah,* the principal source for Youth Aliyah funds, to turn some of the funds to this use; it was arranged that

* At the convention of November, 1935, Mrs. Edward Jacobs, president, presented a plan whereby Hadassah, the Women's Zionist Organization of America, would become the agent in America for the collection of funds for Youth Aliyah. The proposal was accepted enthusiastically.

Photo by Tim Gidal

Greeting youth from Bulgaria, who had been on the road for months, making their way to Palestine

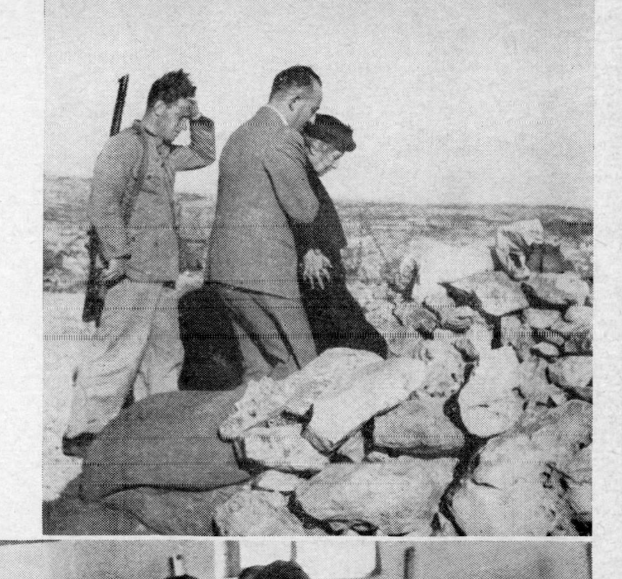

At Maale HaHamisha, founded during period of Arab rioting, 1936-39; accompanied by Hans Beyth and young guard

Photo by Tim Gidal

At Sedjera, with Professor Norman Bentwich and Hans Beyth, discussing possibility of placing a group of young people, 1943

Photo by Tim Gidal

Photo by Tim Gidal

On tour—at Matzubah, October, 1942

Photo by Tim Gidal

Greeting young arrivals from Austria, Kiryat Anavim, 1938

Visiting Kfar Gileadi, northern settlement, with Hans Beyth

Photo by Tim Gidal

At City Hall, New York, 1936, to receive the key to the city—Rabbi Stephen S. Wise and Mayor Fiorello H. LaGuardia

Photo by Acme Newspictures, Inc. Courtesy Hadassah

During 1920's, in living room of the little stone house, Jerusalem

Courtesy Hadassah

sixty children from Palestinian slums should be settled on farms—sixty fortunate ones out of the thousands unschooled, undernourished and unguided.

From Europe came heartbreaking accounts of the attempts of those trapped to break out of the iron ring. Of the eight thousand children deported from the Rumanian provinces of Bukowina and Bessarabia to South Russia, three thousand had perished, four thousand were in a huge orphanage in Mogilev, and the remaining one thousand were roaming the villages, "picking up" a living. The women of Rumania were doing what they could to send clothing, shoes, food and medicine to the orphanage. The children were so reduced in health that they would need months of care before they could be transferred to Palestine.

During the summer of '44 four groups of children and youth made their way into Palestine, emaciated and in rags. Their starting point, three years earlier, had been Transdniestria in the Ukraine.

Emissaries went out of Palestine on hazardous missions behind enemy lines and into other danger zones. One of these, Wilfrid Israel, was lost when the plane carrying him was shot down. Another, Enzo Sereni, son of King Victor Immanuel's personal physician, parachuted into enemy territory, was captured and executed at Dachau.*

Mazal Mosseri, who had lived in Egypt for years and was familiar with the Arab tongue and the Arab people, offered her services to Miss Szold. Rumors, unsubstantiated, but too many and too consistent to be ignored, were coming out of Iraq; the rumors concerned the aftermath of a revolution which had broken out there. The pro-British Regent

* The disastrous losses among British and American airmen during the raids on the Ploesti had revealed fatal weakness in the British Intelligence Service. Among the Jews of Palestine the British sought and found many volunteers for this most dangerous of services.

and the Premier had both been driven out and replaced by Rashid Ali al-Gailani, a German sympathizer and partner of the ex-Mufti of Jerusalem who had fled to Iraq for protection, then gone on to his friends in Germany. It was the period when the Japanese were driving westward, the Germans eastward, in the hope of joining forces. The revolt in Iraq was designed to further this plan.

At stake was the entire Middle East theatre, including the Mosul oil-fields, the Suez Canal, access to India, and British prestige. British reenforcements, rushed from Palestine and Basra (those from Palestine were spearheaded by Jews), forced the capitulation of the Iraqi rebels. Rashid Ali and his lieutenant Fawzi el-Kawukji* fled beforc the entering columns and escaped to Germany.

On the heels of their defeat their disappointed followers in Bagdad fell upon the Jewish minority. The cry raised against them was that they were British sympathizers. One official investigation reported that in one night of murder and looting one hundred and twenty Jews had been killed, many hundreds wounded. Figures varied. Sir Kinahan Cornwallis, the British Ambassador, mentioned two thousand as the number killed. A later official count gave the figure as seven hundred.

Mrs. Mosseri's plan was to go to Iraq, get what information she could and arrange, if possible, to get some children out of the country. Entry into Iraq was closed to her on two counts—she was a journalist; she was a Jewess. The British consuls to whom she applied refused aid and accused her of creating difficulties between the two governments. Nevertheless she went, after a forced wait of five months, with documents certifying that she was an archaeologist. With her she took letters of introduction to Christians, Moslems, and Jews, requesting permission for

* The same who led the invasion of Syrian troops into Palestine in 1948.

her to visit the sites and monuments of antiquity. She devoted the long waiting period to a study of Iraq history and archaeology. Traveling on trains crowded with soldiers, herself the only woman on board, she visited the towns of Iraq—Bagdad, Mosul, Kirkuk, Basra and others. At one point she was identified by an Arab fellow-journalist who recognized her name; but for some reason or other she was not given up to the authorities. Six weeks of contact with the Jews of Iraq enabled her to bring back confirmation of the rumors and to gather a few children—very few, for just as foreign Jews were forbidden to enter Iraq, so those within were denied permission to leave. The only condition on which an Iraqi Jew could leave the country was by the posting of a $20,000 bond. Boys of fifteen and sixteen, often without the knowledge of their parents, attempted to cross the border and make for Palestine.

In Europe and in Asia the drama of escape was enacted and reenacted, the hopes of all converging on Palestine. Sometimes the actors found their haven, even though the haven turned out to be an internment camp at Athlit. At other times the haven they found was the bottom of black waters.

There was the *Salvador* which foundered on December 12, 1940, in the Sea of Marmora. No one knows how many were on board, the figures given varying between two hundred and fifty and three hundred and fifty. The Turkish authorities, in accordance with their own entry regulations, refused to admit any refugees except those in transit to other countries, and these unfortunates had no visas for Palestine, or for any port of this world. A storm at sea wrecked their vessel: one hundred and twenty-three bodies were recovered.

In November, 1940, a number of refugees who had

escaped death and the threat of death arrived at Haifa, by different routes, in small ships. None of them had visas. By order of the Palestine government, eighteen hundred were placed aboard the *Patria,* to be deported, whether to the island of Mauritius or elsewhere they did not know. They knew only that, having reached the shore of Palestine, they were not to be permitted to set foot on it. Their friends were there, eager to welcome them; some among those friends, desperate in their grief and anger, conceived a desperate remedy. On November 25 an explosion shook the boat; slowly it keeled over and capsized. Rowboats in the harbor, manned by willing hands, pulled out the passengers. Those caught below decks (by some blunder), two hundred and fifty of them, never had a chance.

The most ghastly of the disasters was the sinking of the *Struma* on February 24, 1942. Nearly eight hundred refugees from Rumania and Bulgaria, who had been on the road for months, had chartered the boat at the Rumanian port of Constanza. The passengers had been assured by the agents that it was seaworthy, that it had a new engine, that four hundred certificates for Palestine were awaiting them in Turkey. In point of fact it was a cattle boat built for service on the Danube—a fifty-foot Bulgarian-owned vessel of one-hundred-eighty tons, old, leaky, unseaworthy. On December 15 it entered Istanbul waters; conditions on board were desperate. With accommodations for about one hundred passengers, the *Struma* was carrying eight hundred; one hundred and fifty of them were children under sixteen. There was no proper water supply, no heating arrangements, or electricity; there was only one toilet.

The Turkish authorities refused permission to land. The captain notified the port officials that his ship was in no condition for further travel. For more than two months it remained at Istanbul while the Jewish Agency and the American Jewish Joint Distribution Committee continued frantic and unavailing efforts to secure entry permits from the Palestine government. There was no question in this case of exceeding the legal immigration quota. The government held in its possession three thousand unallotted certificates—could not some of these be assigned to the eight hundred on the *Struma*? The government was adamant. The "reasons" given were: 1)- there might be enemy agents among the passengers; 2)- the food supply in Palestine was inadequate.

In reply to the first argument the Jewish Agency suggested that all passengers be interned and thoroughly investigated before being released. In reply to the second argument they submitted the information that two-thirds of the passengers were able-bodied, and prepared to work or to fight; Palestine needed both workers and fighters. And if the food was ample for Christian refugees from Czechoslovakia and Poland, who were coming in by the thousands without let or hindrance, it could be stretched for the few hundreds of the *Struma*, who were too old or too young to be self-supporting. The Joint Distribution Committee was prepared to cover the costs of transportation and to advance L6000 for their care in Palestine.

Nothing could move the British officials. These passengers had left their countries without the necessary visas—a reprehensible breach of etiquette which the officials could in no way condone. The refugees could go back to Rumania, back to the Nazi concentration camps and the Nazi ovens.

Finally, to a limited extent, there was gracious relenting; as a special act of mercy the one hundred and fifty children on board would be admitted, as wards of Youth Aliyah. The cables flew. Too late! A Turkish tug had towed the

Struma out to open waters. In the open sea something happened. According to some accounts the boat struck a floating mine. Others reported that it was torpedoed by a Nazi submarine. Another conjecture came of mass suicide. A report to Washington, submitted by the American Emergency Committee for Zionist Affairs, stated that the boat simply went to pieces as soon as it reached open water. There was one survivor.

Not every episode ended in tragedy. More fortunate were the individuals and the groups who found asylum among Christian people, in private homes and in monasteries. Singularly fortunate was the group of young people admitted to Denmark in the early weeks of the war. Danish Christian circles, in particular the League for Peace and Freedom, were deeply interested in looking after these children. They were received in the homes of farmers with whose families they lived and worked. Their relation with the Danes was that of cherished friends, almost of family members. When the opportunity came and the way to Palestine was opened for them, via Sweden, Finland, and Russia, their foster parents begged them to remain. The children had been happy in their temporary homes, happy in their work, in the associations they had formed, in the cultured atmosphere of these farming homesteads where the adults attended lecture courses, the children went to the folk high schools, and the reading of literature, the study of science and history were a part of daily life.

Meanwhile the Jewish children had met regularly for study and discussion of Palestinian matters. When their hosts argued and pleaded with them to remain, pointed to their uncertain future in Palestine, and affirmed their own willingness to keep them and care for them, the children could not be persuaded to give up their plans.

Commenting on their experience, Miss Szold said: "The

impression left upon my mind by the talks with the two groups regarding their Danish sojourn was that here an episode had occurred which could not be allowed to fall into the limbo of forgotten things. Our memory, alas, is filled to the point of choking with horrors, savagery, and destruction of civilized standards. Should we not reserve at least a small place in which to store a narrative like this testifying to the humanity and culture of a group? For instance, I was deeply impressed by the following:

"When the Danish farmers sought from the children an explanation of their national hopes, they said: 'See, we have received you here from purely humanitarian motives; do they not suffice?' And when apparently they were beaten in the argument, the farmers said: 'At all events, since we received you from humanitarian motives, you ought to remember, when you constitute yourselves a nation, to receive others, strangers, from humanitarian motives.' My remark to our groups was that that sentiment the Danes learned from our Bible which enjoins kindness to the stranger."

Teheran! to the world in general it is a city in Iran. In Palestine the name signifies an event, not a geographical location.

In the late summer and fall of 1942, the Jewish community of Palestine, already emotionally overcharged by the events of the war years, was thrown into a fever of excitement by reports that seeped through of a mass movement of hundreds of Polish children. The children formed only one section of a straggling mass of 14,000—there were civilians and soldiers, adults and children, Christians and Jews who, throughout the three years since the tearing apart of Poland by Germany and Russia, had been wandering through forests and villages, across deserts and rivers.

According to the first reports, the children, four hundred and forty of them, were at Pahlevi, an Iranian port on the Caspian Sea. In the course of the following weeks, report after report raised the number of the Jewish children to five hundred, to six hundred, then to eight hundred, and finally to nine hundred and thirty-three—all known by name.

The children ranged in age from a year and a half to eighteen years. They were starved, half-naked, eaten by vermin, disease-ridden. One hundred and seventy-nine were accompanied by their parents; others were held together by Zionist youth leaders. By November the children had all been gathered in a camp near Teheran, together with the other thousands of refugees, and were being cared for by the Polish Red Cross and by the Joint Distribution Committee.

The last leg of their journey, from Teheran to Palestine, was a long one. Instead of the comparatively short, direct route by rail across the desert, the children had to be transported south by rail to Karachi, India, then carried by troopship across the Arabian Sea and up the Red Sea to Suez, where they boarded the train for Palestine. The reason for the long detour? The anti-Zionist principles of Moslem Iraq, which refused passage across its territory to these young wanderers who sought the Home which had been pledged to them by international authority.

At the Red Sea port a contingent of Jewish military engineers had word of their coming. Excitement seized the camp. In the few hours that remained before the expected arrival of the transport, funds were collected, provisions bought, and gift packages readied by assembly-line technique, to be thrust into each child's hand. In each package was a printed slip, reading:

We, a unit of Palestinian Jewish soldiers doing its work on alien soil, have had the great good fortune to be the first to welcome you home and to give you the traditional blessing of our people: "Peace be unto you." Blessed be you in your coming, young brothers and sisters. It is you and such as you who give meaning and purpose to our participation in this war. You are the reason for which we throw ourselves into danger and hardship. Your coming is only a token of the coming of multitudes after you. It forces us and encourages us to labor beyond our strength for the salvation of the others to follow you.

The men cried like children as they filled the paper bags, cut and sewed flags for the children, and prepared banners with the motto, "And the children shall return unto their borders." They cried in grief for what had been; in joy for what would be.

In the bag thrust into her hand one child found this note:

To You, Child That Goes Up to the Land:

This is the name by which I wish to call you. I will not call you a refugee child for, from this moment on, you are a builder and a pioneer. You will work in the Land and build the Land and love it. And so you will forget the cup of grief from which you have drunk to the full.

A Jewish Soldier

From the first Jewish station reached, Rehobot, the route of the train was a triumphal progress. Welcoming crowds, carrying placards with the greeting, "Blessed be the newcomers to the land of our fathers," bore down on the train, showering offerings of flowers and goodies. The village swarmed with three thousand of them, come to greet, as their own children, not as miserable orphans, those who had never known, or long forgotten, compassion and kindness. The children wept, but the welcomers answered with songs of joy. Then there was no more weeping, and all joined together in singing the songs of Zion.

The Youth Aliyah Bureau now faced a complex of problems such as it had never faced before. For the first units there had been months of preparation in Europe and in Palestine. The groundwork had been slowly and solidly laid, so solidly that few changes in method had had to be made for the later groups. From time to time, during the war, children had wandered in and become wards of Youth Aliyah, but always in comparatively small groups.

The age range of the newcomers constituted a part of the problem, which was both administrative and financial. In general, Youth Aliyah wards had ranged in age from fifteen to seventeen years; the number of children below fifteen had been small in proportion to the whole, and these had been assigned, not to collectives, but either to child institutions or to private homes. In the Teheran group, however, eighty percent were less than fifteen years of age and would therefore require guardianship over a long period.

In other respects, too, there were radical differences between this and the pre-war groups. While the earlier candidates for settlement had been required to pass severe physical and psychological tests, the new arrivals were in a deplorable state of health; for their dental treatment alone the initial outlay came to L3000. Again, instead of being well-equipped, these brought their rags. And they came, the youngest with no memory of home life, the older ones having forgotten the traditions of civilized living. Few of them had had formal schooling of any kind.

The excitement among the public continued for months. The children were besieged by visitors—some sought news of relatives; some hoped to find survivors of their own families among the children; some came to express sympathy; some to satisfy their curiosity. Miss Szold was compelled to issue an appeal requesting the public to refrain from visiting the children's camps and homes and disrupting the new routine of their lives.

One particular problem, always a thorny one for Youth Aliyah, now loomed large. Primarily it arose out of the fact that the Jewish settlement in Palestine, instead of maintaining a national, non-party type of school, fosters a tri-partite system, based on political divisions within the Zionist Organization. The General Zionist center and the Labor Lefts maintain systems of secular education in which the Bible is studied as history and literature. The right-wing Mizrahi maintain a school system which stresses the study of the Talmud and insists on all the minutiae of rigid orthodox observance. Although known as the religious group, the Mizrahi actually constitute a political faction rather than the religious element in the community. Many observant Jews refuse to send their children to Mizrahi schools because they do not wish them to become either the objects or the agents of party propaganda.

Each young immigrant among the earlier comers had been affiliated with a particular Zionist group, representing a specific ideology. On arriving in Palestine his assignment to a settlement had been in accordance with his professed affiliation in the belief that harmony of purpose would make for harmony in living.

The system had never worked perfectly, largely because the orthodox wing had failed to establish agricultural settlements either of the collective or the small-holder type. When Youth Aliyah initiated its rescue work, only one agricultural settlement, Rodges, was open to orthodox youth. The labor groups, on the other hand, were so far in the lead that, by 1933, their settlements were scattered through the length and breadth of the land.

The young people from Germany, aware of this situation and desperately anxious to leave Europe, sometimes concealed the fact that their home backgrounds had been orthodox. Within two weeks of the arrival of the first group in 1934, Miss Szold, herself a life-long observer of law and ritual, had sensed the situation and was conveying her suspicions to the German office of Youth Aliyah. She had received the impression, she wrote, that the parents of the group laid stress on Jewish observances; she wanted to be sure that the young people knew in advance the attitude of the settlements towards religious tradition. The children must be made aware, she warned her colleagues in Germany, of the serious implications in the change from observance to disregard of tradition. Again and again, in her letters to the German office, she emphasized the importance of making this point.

She recognized also that her own position in not insisting on rigid observance was somewhat anomalous. We see the process of soul-searching in a letter written to Mrs. Edward Jacobs, then president of the American Hadassah: "I do not think that because a Jew comes to live in Palestine he must allow himself to be forced into the acceptance of a religious form of life. That attitude to my mind is a Hitler attitude. Suppose Ain Harod were to agree to observe the Sabbath as I believe it should be observed, and the dietary laws, but conformed only outwardly without any feeling for the hallowed values involved, would such acquiescence make it a trustworthy teacher of youth?

The Mizrahi system finds such a course acceptable; I do not; as a matter of fact, in my conception of Judaism, the demand is not in its spirit. However, I do agree that the question should arise in my mind whether, seeing that the Jewish religious tradition is sacred to me, I am true to myself when I agree to be the instrument, the hand, that places Jewish children in homes in which traditional Judaism is not inculcated, not even in unorthodox form. The question is not strange to me. I put it to myself and I answered it affirmatively, because the Youth Aliyah is a humanitarian undertaking. The answer cannot satisfy Rabbi ———. In the case of religion and in the case of the national language, I am prepared to entrust the outcome to life. I know that the losses may be great. Missionarism and inquisitorial practice also involve losses. Weigh one kind against the other."

It had become standard practice for the various groups to send missionary delegates to centers in Europe where the children were being assembled in preparatory camps. Enticements of various kinds were held out to the children by the rival camps in the effort to influence them to demand one or another form of schooling. Eight-year-old Moishele, from whom patient questioning elicited nothing, for he had no recollection of home, of parents, of family, of anything but his name, Moishele announced with decision at the end of the interview, "But I want you to know that I am HaShomer HaZair," naming the extreme left of the Labor Party as his affiliation.

At one settlement the incoming children belonged to five different political groups. They formed five separate cliques, each refusing to associate with the others in work, study or play. With some difficulty the five parent organizations were persuaded to abstain from their "educational" activities for a six-month period. At the end of the six months a well-integrated group of young people were working and playing and studying in full and hearty cooperation.

In the case of the Teheran children preliminary observations had been made by the teachers during the long wait for entry into Palestine. Instead of assigning each child immediately to his point of settlement, Miss Szold determined to continue investigations over an additional period of six weeks, in order to uncover, as far as possible, what the early training in the parental home had been. This information would serve as guide in placing the child. Then, should the miracle occur—the miracle of parents and children reunited—the education of the children would not have been a factor in creating a gap between the generations. Those fourteen years of age and older, matured by their unusual experiences, were allowed to choose their place of settlement.

One of the children's homes, Ahavah (Love), was emptied of its regular occupants to make room for the children from Teheran. Over its door is inscribed the motto: "Love builds worlds; hate destroys them." For one week Miss Szold engaged one after another of four hundred children in personal informal conversation—having first given careful study to the child's record. The conversations lasted five to twenty minutes each.

Family groups of brothers, sisters, cousins, clung together in affection and fear. They said to Miss Szold: "We have too often in our wanderings been separated from each other; we are now separated from our parents; nothing will induce us to part from one another." To Miss Szold this loyalty was the most appealing trait revealed by the group which, in other respects, showed hardness, selfishness, and suspicion.

The girls, while they averred that their homes had been observant, insisted obstinately upon going to the non-observant settlements and institutions. Argument that the probable wishes of their dead or missing parents should be considered failed to move them. Nor would they be persuaded when Miss Szold pointed out that it might be their duty to relinquish their own wishes for the sake of the younger members of their families. "I have to confess," she admitted, "that I succeeded in not a single case."

The girls' principal argument was that there were greater educational opportunities for girls in the non-observant than in the orthodox groups. The attitude of those parents who accompanied their children bore out this contention; not one parent requested that his child be placed in an orthodox institution. Refusing to exercise any form of moral or physical compulsion, Miss Szold placed the children, in accordance with their wishes, in non-orthodox settlements. But her respect for their personalities cost her dear. Turmoil seized the orthodox communities; the air seethed with controversy and crackled with charges.

Miss Szold had always hoped that the rabbis would give up their rigidity, and renew the methods of adjusting law to life which had been a distinctive feature of the rabbinic period of Jewish history. She found that the rabbis remained rigid: "I have had occasion to observe that anew in Palestine—and the corroding influences of modern life multiply." Now this view was reenforced by hard personal experience. The attitude of the rabbis on the question of the children's education—they suggested a mathematical division of fifty-fifty between the orthodox and non-orthodox settlements—revolted her conscience. To one friend Miss Szold described her experiences of this period as a series of psychic and mental shocks. Even to her sister Bertha she could not go into the details of the struggle, and what it meant to her. "In part," she wrote, "I was too naive; in part, I fear, too sure of my rectitude. I thought, it appears, that after twenty-four years of life in Palestine, during which I have been able to keep my skirts free of partisan strife, I was fire-proof. Events proved me wrong."

Quite uninfluenced by all that had happened—the discussions, the recriminations, the demands—she conducted the examinations of the children as she had always conducted them. "I may add," she wrote, "not in order to demonstrate honesty and allegiance to truth, but simply to complete the picture, that after I finished the examination, the representatives of the religious groups expressed great satisfaction."

The satisfaction was short-lived. A few months thereafter Miss Szold was writing: "The head and front of my offending is two-horned. First, I examined only four hundred, not the whole seven hundred and sixteen, due to my illness. As it was, I got out of a real and serious sick-bed to do the questioning. I had to drive myself cruelly to stand on my feet, let alone that I had to do the questioning tactically, as far removed from a Torquemada act as possible. The questioning had to be completed so that the temporary camps could be liquidated before Pesach. The second horn was that I had appointed leaders from all currents in the community. The demand of Rabbi ——— and his sympathizers was that all the leaders were to be from the orthodox communities. In other words, I was to administer a slap in the face to the large sections of the public which, in the course of ten years, had helped the Youth Aliyah Bureau to bring to Palestine and settle 8500 boys and girls, among them a fair percentage of the orthodox. Rabbi ——— could not see eye to eye with me. In America he has the active assistance of Rabbi ———. What neither of them realizes is that the children themselves put up a violent resistance to placement in orthodox settlements and institutions due to the ugly, vicious propaganda carried on among the camps."

The sadness and bitterness engendered in Miss Szold by these experiences had to find expression. "Where were they," she wrote, "when the work of building began, and where were they when the youth immigration began? They appeared on the scene late and unprepared, yet with maximal demands. The neglect of generations is a heavy sin that cannot be atoned for in a single generation, and at the hands of one old, weak woman. Why do they lay on me the burden of expiation for their sins? I can bear no more." To another friend she made the statement that only her deep religious feeling prevented her from becoming anti-orthodox in spirit. In letter after letter she explained in patient detail the minutiae of the situation to detractors who set upon her from all quarters of the Zionist world. The ordeal left its searing mark on body, mind and spirit.

Her gratitude went out to her staff for its unswerving support and to the leftist groups who showed themselves not unsympathethic to her own demands for conformity to religious practices; and who encouraged her by their confidence in her honesty of purpose and her judgment on the religious question. But the spiritual hurt was deep—deepest in that she saw flouted, by the very forces that should have had it in most sacred keeping, the lofty ethics of the Judaism she had always served.

The Ihud controversy also (treated in an earlier chapter) was now coming to a head. Each situation aggravated the other and emphasized the cleavage in spirit and method between Miss Szold and the ruling forces in the Organization. But where a vital principle was involved, not even her deference for duly constituted authority could make her give way an inch.

Thus when the Jewish Agency, ignoring her as liaison officer for child immigration, asked the government for entry certificates for 50,000 children, she refused to go along with the demand. With the funds in hand and in prospect, 10,000 was the utmost she could honestly undertake responsibility for. Possibly, in time, another 10,000 might be provided for: "As soon as I was told that the Agency had informed the government—not in consonance with my opinion!—that we were ready to care for 50,000 children, I wrote to the Agency that then the Agency must be the ultimate guarantor." Because of her stand in the matter the Jewish Agency saw fit to denounce Miss Szold as a minimalist: "Do you think," they said, "that an undertaking of this nature should be entrusted to a dissident minimalist?"

The intrusion of partisan politics into her purely pedagogic approach led to a radical change in organization. The Youth Aliyah Bureau, hitherto autonomous, now had to submit its policies to the review and approval of the Jewish Agency. In the deliberations preceding the change Miss Szold had had no invitation to take part.

With the arrival of the Teheran group still other aspects of Miss Szold's pedagogic approach were called in question. Youth Aliyah had never used the usual paraphernalia of personal sponsorships as a means of stimulating fund collection, with its accompaniments of photographs and human interest stories. In 1936 Miss Szold had written: "We have succeeded in banishing from our relations to the Youth Aliyah every tincture of philanthropy. We all realize that abstention from sponsorships might mean a loss in the collection of funds . . . We are prepared to sustain that loss in view of the productive advantages accompanying a purely educational attitude." When, in 1943 and 1944, the question of personal sponsoring was brought up again, she declared that the children were the wards of the nation: "If they feel gratitude, they must show it towards the nation in the upbuilding of Palestine."

Neither personalities nor stories were to be exploited to serve the uses of publicity. "As a matter of fact," she answered one inquirer, "there is a story to tell about ———, but I am not going to tell it. It is of such a character that I cannot permit it to be used, even if his name does not appear. By now you will have learned that I have what some people would call a "complex" on the subject of the soul of the child entrusted to me. People here frequently question the children who came from Poland via Teheran about all the gruesome details of all they had experienced. In all my talks with the children from Teheran, never have I asked a single question. The ——— story is also sacred to me. I cannot tell it."

For similar reasons she set her face against the presentation to selected children of gift packages from unknown donors. Gifts to individuals, setting some in a position of special privilege, were apt to affect the children's relations with one another.

In other ways, too, these lost waifs were made to feel themselves the wanted children of a loving and watchful mother. Not theirs the carefully mended garments cast off by the charitable. The clothing and shoes they donned, their outer garments and undergarments, were bright, new and well made. New clothes were the external manifestation of new lives. In Miss Szold's eyes, the feeling of self-respect and personal dignity that these clothes brought fully justified the expense involved.

For the Teheran children in particular special attempts were made to provide close personal relations with older people or with family groups in the settlement. Children were informally "adopted" into family units with whom they spent their leisure; birthdays were observed by celebrations and the giving of gifts; older boys and girls became big brothers and sisters to younger ones.

In spite of all that could be done, the process of adjustment to ordered living was not easy. While the younger children slipped into the new life with little difficulty, it was harder for the teen-agers. They had trouble in concentrating on their studies and in mastering the intricacies of the new language; even sitting still for any length of time required a definite effort of will. Moreover, lack of knowledge and of skills made them uneasy in the presence of the Palestinian youth. Past experiences were a barrier between them and the others. Some decided to leave their groups and make their own way; others remained to grope their way to understanding and serenity. How pitiful the struggle was is revealed in the words set down by one of these children:

> If . . . a button is missing from my trousers, if the color of my overalls has faded, if I receive socks with darns when I want socks without darns, then everything . . . loses value in my eyes. And is this right? It shows lack of faith. But how should we have faith? Did the prison camps, the constant fear, hunger and barbarity around us teach us to have faith? We didn't even trust our own brothers. What I held in my hand, in my own hand, that alone was mine. It is clear that the new road is not easy for us; it is difficult to expect us to have faith. But if we cannot overcome our lack of faith in small matters, how can we have faith in the

important big issues that affect fundamentally our future lives together?

The last word on the subject of Teheran belongs of right to Henrietta Szold. On February 18, 1944, she exults: "Today I am also celebrating an anniversary; today a year ago the Polish children arrived from Teheran. It is an anniversary to be celebrated . . . The children who, we thought, would present problems of the most difficult kind, have been perfectly normal, happy, big and little human beings. And how they have acquired Hebrew!"

17. *Youth Aliyah—Postgraduate*

"Can you imagine a colonization scheme more beautiful?"

IN GIVING the foregoing account of an enterprise covering eleven years, many details have necessarily been omitted, but it is impossible to leave the subject without some mention, however brief, of the "postgraduate" activities of Youth Aliyah wards.

The "coming of age" of the first group, in 1936, coincided with the beginning of disturbances* which were to go on for three and a half years until the outbreak of World War II. Henrietta Szold knew and respected the desire of the young people to identify themselves with the community. Just as she herself could not forego taking her share in danger when she undertook her trips in armed convoys—"The more reason for me to go and not some one younger, for I have lived my life"—so she could not say to them: "Hide yourselves, take care of your own skins, pay no attention to what is happening to others." They stood on guard with their elders, sharing the common danger and anxiety. Fortunately there were no fatalities among them, and there was only one serious casualty.

Notwithstanding the fact that the entire period was marked by waves of arson and murder, the young graduates proceeded with their program of settlement. During

* See Chapter 11.

the three-and-a-half years forty-nine settlements struck root in the soil. In some of these Youth Aliyah graduates were the nucleus; they were represented in practically all. By the end of 1947 these staunch young men and women had established themselves at isolated and dangerous points from the northern mountains to the southern desert.

Kfar Szold, named after their beloved director, lies low on a mountain ridge, the top of which marks the Syrian boundary. Manara,* surrounded by Arab villages, occupies the crest of a lofty height. The search for water at Manara was long. For years the only water was a trickle which had to be used for drinking; for cooking, cleaning and irrigating, use was made of rain water stored in cisterns, supplemented by supplies trucked uphill over rough country from a village five miles away.

In Matzubah water flowed after seven years of toil and lean living. The settlers sold their hand-loomed fabrics and worked in small-holders' villages for a day's wages. Their courage and self-confidence stilled Miss Szold's doubts and forebodings. There were minor catastrophes in their history as when, in one night, one hundred and seventy sapling plums were uprooted; there had been no quarrel with the Arab villagers, no signs of enmity, nothing to account for the malicious destruction.

Beth Eshel, pinpoint in a waste of hot desert sand, experimented in the chemical growing of vegetables, and harvested eight crops of potatoes where one crop was harvested before. And at Beth HaAravah the curse of the salt wastes was washed away—washed away by the sweat and strain of boys and girls barely out of their teens, who were determined to redeem a few acres more so that others might join them in finding food for their bodies and peace for their souls.

* Now Ramim.

When the call to arms came, in 1939, the Youth Aliyah boys strode into the ranks to the number of two thousand—more than half of those eligible—resentful only that they were assigned to labor squadrons and not accorded the high privilege of risking their lives in battle under their own flag. Many attested their convictions with their lives. A transport company was torpedoed at night off the African coast. The boys stirred the hearts of their rescuers who found them swimming about in the waters, singing their Hebrew songs. Twenty-five of the singers went down.

To some of her wards Miss Szold refused the right to enlist, either because they were too young, or because they had come into the land too recently and were not sufficiently familiar with its language or with conditions in the country. She warned them to be sure, before coming to a final decision, that they were not prompted to enlist by a spirit of adventure or by the wish to shirk daily tasks. To help them reach a decision, she addressed them in these words:

> We all, old and young, know that the time calls for the last sacrifice, so that those who come after us may not be deprived of the highest purpose of life; and the young men are called upon to make the most complete sacrifice. From you it is asked that you give even your life . . . Your resolve to heed the call is sure proof that you are filled with the conviction that if this precious heritage of humanity disappears, the death sentence is proclaimed against the Jews, body and soul. The war is doubly a Jewish concern. It affects us as members of humanity and also as Jews . . .
>
> In many ways the land of the Bible in which we live is the last fortress of the Jewish people. There are Jews who believe that, if this fortress is captured today

by our enemy, the whole Jewish people would be so injured by the loss that it could not recover. My personal faith is otherwise. I believe in the strength of the remnant of Israel even if the remnant is small. Only it must be adequate . . . My counsel and questioning have but one single purpose: to bring home to you that you may not just say, generally and dogmatically, to one another: "Join the army," or "Do not enroll," or "Do it only under this or that condition." Where there is no conscription, each individual must search himself deeply and form his own conviction.

Shortly before his death Hans Beyth, on returning from one of his trips, counted off on his fingers graduate after graduate whom he had run into in the course of a few evening hours—the driver who had taken him to Afuleh; the owner of the hotel at which he spent the night; the nurse in the X-ray room at the Emek Hospital. And so his recital went on to show how these lads and lasses, a few years earlier helpless and dependent victims of outrageous circumstance, had worked themselves into the warp and woof of the land.

By the end of 1947 twenty-two thousand boys and girls had been rescued by this agency. It is a record of which every one concerned may well be proud, not least, the donors in all parts of the world—the organizations in the United States, Canada, England, South Africa, South America, and other regions, the Eddie Cantors* and the Miss Mackubins†—who helped in the rescue of souls and in the colonization scheme, of which its director asked; "Can you imagine a colonization scheme more beautiful?"

* Eddie Cantor has been active for many years in raising funds for Youth Aliyah.

† See page 241.

18. *For the Sake of the Child*

"As you see I am not yet too old to dream dreams"

ASKED what might be considered the crown of Miss Szold's achievements, most persons would probably point to Youth Aliyah. Some would question that view, holding that the American Hadassah was a still more important creation since, without this channel by means of which she established structure after structure, none of her achievements in Palestine would have been possible. As to Miss Szold's own answer there need be no speculation. She gave it in no uncertain terms, in accord with neither of the answers suggested above.

It was at the end of 1941 that she laid her plan before her public. That morning, December 21, her eighty-first birthday had been celebrated informally by her associates in the Youth Aliyah office. There had been no tinge of the official about this celebration; this was her family who were joining her in a breakfast of coffee and cake, served on a flower-decked table, indulging in humorous skits, of meaning only in the intimate circle of the office. The usual delegation of youngsters from the Children's Village of Meir Shfeya was there, come to present her, according to their custom, with home-grown roses, equal in number to the number of her years.

Following the celebration she proceeded in high spirits

to a conference of social workers and laid her plan before them in its final, legal form. In desperate fear lest it fail for lack of understanding, she cried out to them: "This once, I beg of you what I have never asked before. This once, if you don't understand, believe!"

It was not in Miss Szold's nature to demand belief; all the years of her life she had made her sole appeal to the understanding of her colleagues. But at eighty-one there is little time ahead in which to build up understanding, and the vision before her brooked no denial, for the vision she saw was—unity for her people.

Eighteen years earlier she had told an American audience that there was work to be done in Zion that could not be done with money, work that would take not one generation, but two and three and four. "I want to warn you against haste," she had said then. "It is work that cannot be done over night, and if it were done over night, it would be valueless. It would not make us one people, one homogeneous section of the human race, who have a particular piece of work to do. Unless we have patience, we will destroy the work of our hands."

How to make one out of many—that was the besetting internal problem of Jewish Palestine, just as the relationship with Arabs was its besetting external problem. At fifty-nine, beginning her active work there, she had seen on every hand heterogeneity. There had not been so much as a common language. The women, struggling to organize, listened to addresses in halting Hebrew, addresses which had to be translated into various languages—into Yiddish for those recently from East European countries; into Ladino, the local Spanish patois spoken by the native Sephardi women; into Arabic for those coming from the Middle East. Some of those present, unable to follow any of these languages, had to depend upon the whispered explanations of their more linguistically accomplished neighbors. "Never," one of the assembly was heard to murmur, "can unity be produced out of such elements."

Language was only one of the external manifestations of cultural heterogeneity. Jews from Kurdistan, from Morocco, from Bokhara, Syria, Iraq, Iran, Turkey, Yemen, were bringing with them ways of living and modes of thinking which were at variance with one another, and certainly at variance with those coming from Europe—who were themselves the carriers of more or less sharply differentiated cultures. Primitive Orientalism was colliding head on with the twentieth century, and trouble was in the wake of the collision.

Palestine Jewry could no longer boast that all its children received at least elementary schooling. Through the neglect, the ignorance or the poverty of their parents, the young of the Oriental groups were, in no small numbers, denied their Jewish birthright of education. In earlier days the naturally high birth rate had been balanced by a heavy infant mortality. This was now being cut into by good hospital service, and by the pre-natal and post-natal care given by Hadassah and other health agencies. Result—a constant increase in the proportion of underprivileged young people, at odds with their parents, living in crowded, unsanitary quarters, untrained to meet the challenge of a modern, twentieth-century civilization, unable to stand on firm ground, either economically or culturally. Intellectually immature and emotionally unstable, they drifted into trouble with the law and created a major delinquency problem.

Long-settled communities have their own ways of combatting such problems. School attendance can be required by law; special educational agencies and institutions can be established; child labor can be controlled. It may be a menace in their case also, but a menace capable of a greater degree of control. In a young community, struggling to find its feet, the menace of juvenile delinquency is that of a growing cancer, threatening to engulf the whole body politic.

Henrietta Szold's sharp sense of the interplay of forces affecting the weal and woe of her people brought her early to the realization of this menace. Playgrounds, first established by her in 1922, were an early expression of that realization. The establishment of schools for vocational training was another attempt to deal with the problem. Other welfare activities were begun by various agencies; they were initiated, for the most part, because of some one's chance interest and were often haphazardly planned, prematurely begun and carelessly executed. There was no centralization of related activities, no public supervision of institutions, no coordinated system for collecting and administering funds.

It was to the end of avoiding such haphazard undertakings that Miss Szold conceived the plan for a central forum, with experienced personnel who would investigate projects of one kind or another, and determine what should be undertaken.

The heart of every project was to be the child—in the first place, for the improvement of his own physical and mental health; in the second place, as the means for rehabilitating the body politic. To be sure, all social welfare redounds to the benefit of the public at large. Miss Szold hoped, however, that the appeal of the child would act as leaven in the seething partisanships of the community—political groups striving for position, religious fundamentalists conflicting with non-conformists, Orientals versus Europeans. Surely, around the child, as around no other possible center, a sense of responsibility would crystallize: the child's needs would become the fulcrum for balancing conflicting interests. With the child and the child's vital interests held unwaveringly in the center of the picture, there would be no room for partisan strife or for the play of small personal ambitions.

The instrumentality through which she proposed to effect her purpose was a central fund for child and youth welfare, known in Hebrew as *LeMaan HaYeled veHaNoar* (For the Sake of the Child and the Youth). This Child and Youth Welfare Foundation, to give it its English title, was the direct outcome of three large gifts—L4000 from the American Hadassah, a gift in honor of Miss Szold on her seventieth birthday; L4000 presented by the National Council in honor of her seventy-fifth birthday, and $25,-000, also from Hadassah, given as a memorial to the late Felix M. Warburg. Twenty years of thinking and planning had gone into the slow shaping of the plan. During those years, with some such end in view, Miss Szold had carefully and lovingly hoarded many gifts of small sums from friends and well-wishers. Now her hoarded treasure swelled the larger sums. Altogether the endowment fund amounted to L16,000.

The beginnings would necessarily be small. To this Miss Szold had no objection; in fact, she considered it an advantage because it would enable the trustees of the fund to feel their way slowly, and also because the need for adding to the fund would be an occasion for disseminating information and creating public opinion. To the doubters who protested that nothing could be accomplished with small means, she pointed to the violets on her desk. "You see these violets," she said. "First the seed must take root, and the roots grow deep and strong. Nothing appears on the surface for a long time, then suddenly the fields are fragrant with their odor and their bloom delights the eye." To her mind *slow* growth was an essential element of success.

Before the constitution was drawn up in final form, five full years had been devoted to its preparation. Part of the preparation had been a study of child welfare organizations as conducted in other countries. The model finally adopted was the Pro Juventute of Switzerland, with changes made necessary by the fact that the Palestinian organization was a voluntary one while Pro Juventute was an arm of the Swiss government, amply provided for out of government funds, and backed by law.

This same five-year period had served another purpose. True to her educational methods, Miss Szold held many conferences with the corps of professional social workers, discussing with them every article and every phrase of the constitution, weighing the pros and cons of every suggested change, considering the legal, educational, and psychological aspects of every point. The result was an informed body of social workers.

The function stressed for the newly created body was coordination of activities. The first need was a central office; the next, sociological research by a competent staff. On the basis of this research the expenditure of each year's funds was to be determined.

The situation in Palestine has not improved with time. Statistics for 1947 showed that in that year only five percent of children in Oriental groups had completed eight years of elementary school, that the great majority had had not more than five years' schooling. In a few years these groups would comprise about two-thirds of the Jewish population in the country. It was upon this element that the Jewish terrorists of Palestine drew for their dupes and their disciples. In 1947 it was a sight not easily forgotten—these twelve-year-olds, handkerchiefs concealing their features as they engaged in publicity stunts, kiting threatening banners or posting warning placards and stickers, while onlookers dared not interfere, for fear of becoming marked men.

No attempt can be made in this brief presentation to give details of procedure or organization. It may be safely asserted, however, that within a few years of its establishment, LeMaan HaYeled veHaNoar was bringing results: it had trained volunteer forces, published valuable studies, and started important undertakings.

For example, a summer recreation camp for working youth met with marked success. It was established for children of thirteen to sixteen years of age who, because they were earning a living, could not take part in the recreational program of the school system. For these children the camp was a greatly needed relief from working routine—an experience to look forward to for months, and to treasure in their memories.

Miss Szold had once set down the words: "Vision has not failed . . . Unfailing vision is salvation for him who dreams and him who achieves." Unity was her vision, her legacy to her people. The unity she saw was not that of the totalitarians, not the elimination of all conflict of opinion. Up to a certain point she regarded such conflict as healthy; beyond that point it was a sign of sickly disintegration.

Her ends, she knew, would not be attained within the foreseeable future. Her vision swept beyond the years immediately ahead: "I am thinking not of the present, not of National Council, not of Hadassah, not of the moment. I am looking to the morrow and I want to give this to Am Yisrael." She laid the task confidently "upon the people of the 'Messianic hope' the people, that is, which looks forward optimistically into its future and the future of mankind, and is fortified by the conviction that human nature and character are infinitely perfectible." Facing its task with honesty of purpose, with firmness of resolve, Jewish Palestine would effect the "double synthesis, the synthesis between the Jewish past and the Jewish present, and the synthesis among the fragments, the jetsam and flotsam, of world Jewry that make up 'the ingathering of the exiles.' "

The little child would lead them.

In this, which may be thought of as her last will and testament, are the two shining threads that ran through all her thinking and planning—one, the child: the other, unity for the scattered remnant. Here they blend and fuse into one, each giving its own color and life to the other.

19. *By Reason of Strength*

"I don't want sympathy, and thought, and care, and consideration. I want to work"

"LITTLE," and "frail," were terms frequently used in speaking of Henrietta Szold. The terms no doubt applied during the last years of her life, but those who knew her at other times laugh at the notion of frailty in association with her. Though not tall in stature, her full body and physical vigor gave the impression, in her middle years, of a large woman. The robust body lightened with the years, and the flesh was shed as though to keep pace with the shedding of layer upon layer of Victorian reserve, her nineteenth-century heritage.

The length of her regular working day hardly bespoke frailty. When her colleagues on the Palestine Zionist Executive, immediately following their election at an all-night session, asked, "When shall we have our first meeting?" it being then 4 A.M., the answer of the "frail" woman of sixty-seven came promptly: "Now!"

With her short, almost dancing step she easily outdistanced, at seventy-two, her much younger companions. To the young woman who demurred at the idea of a climb to the top of Mount Mizpah on a hot summer day, "Very well, Julia, you stay here. Your father and I will go up." She was seventy-seven when she bested an athletic German who expatiated on the virtues of knee-bending as a limbering exercise. He could do it twelve times, he boasted. "I can do better than that," she said, and proceeded to prove it. The setting-up exercises which followed her morning prayers had kept her limber.

Not many people would have found it possible, as she did at eighty-two, to work all day at Haifa, meeting a ship and interviewing children from 8 A.M. to 3 P.M., attending conferences from 3 P.M. to 11 P.M., then, after an interval of rest, starting out at 4 A.M. for the four-hour drive up to Jerusalem in order to be on time for an 8:15 meeting the following morning. During Miss Szold's last illness a young secretary was chided for her tears and reminded of her friend's advanced age. She answered in perfect sincerity: "I never thought of her as old. She was young when I began working in the office." "How old was she?" "Only seventy-four."

"Tired heart," Dr. Julius Kleeberg told her in the summer of 1938, in explanation of what was actually a serious condition of angina. From that time on her pace was slower; she complained to her sister Bertha that the doctor allowed her only twelve hours of work daily, although what she had to do required at least eighteen. In 1940 an attack of pneumonia left her in weakened condition, with an area of infection in one lung.

The ties that bound her both to her family and to the land of her birth were very strong. Almost from the beginning of her stay in Palestine her thoughts had turned constantly homeward, from the "Oh, dear, if you knew how hard it is on me not to go back," of 1922, to the last of her family letters. At one time, when a decision had to be made, it was largely the influence of Louis D. Brandeis which led her to remain. It was the opinion of Justice Brandeis that Miss Szold's mere presence in Palestine, no matter what task she undertook, was of incalculable importance. Her strong sense of duty, her deference for the views of others, her ability to "rise above the personal"—all impelled her to remain.

For years there stood in her room—mute testimony to her sense of the impermanence of her stay in Palestine—the wardrobe trunk which she had brought with her in 1920, and which she used instead of a chest of drawers. Years later, when her friends gave her a bookcase, she exclaimed: "How could I live without one all these years? Of course it makes me even more homesick for my very own books in storage."

Acknowledging a contribution from the Children's Crusade in America, she wrote to Dorothy Canfield Fisher of her gratitude to a sister movement which originated "in that blessed country that helps refugees and makes none." And when she told friends of Wendell Willkie's visit to her on his trip around the world in 1942, her words were: "A breath of fresh American air came into the room."

The account by one of her correspondents of a piece of public work being conducted in America evoked her admiration. It proved, she said, the validity of one of her pet opinions: "that Americans may not be 'idealists' of the vaunted variety so often held up as models, but instead they have public spirit springing from a sensitive conscience and a noble conception of human living." She often commented on the disrespect of the Palestinians for American Jewry. "The only Americans for whom people in Palestine have any fondness," she said, "are the white leghorns."

In the winter and spring of 1932-33 the homesickness was eased by a visit from her sister, Bertha Szold Levin. It was originally planned that after that visit Miss Szold was to go home for good: "I am going to be coddled by my sisters," she said. The plight of European Jewry put an end to that plan: "I should have felt like a renegade if I had not remained to do my bit."

In 1939 both Bertha and Adele were with her. Instead of being coddled by them, she did the coddling, for both fell ill. Their return to the States—Bertha to rejoin her children and grandchildren, Adele's illness to end in death—marked the last leave-taking.

Each word of home in Bertha's letters stirred memories:

> Rhexia virginica! How long since I have either heard the name or seen the flower.
>
> Your enumeration of the spring blossoms in Eva Leah's woods made me homesick beyond words.
>
> I wish, oh how I wish I could be going over the old household goods with you!
>
> To think of Golden Bantam corn, and fish with flavor, and a walk through ferny woods! It's like hearing the glories of the ancient Temple service and not having the privilege of witnessing them.

Over the fence of the little fruit garden outside her Youth Aliyah office grew a honeysuckle vine; its fragrance filling her room made her dream of home: "Perhaps I shall survive this terrible war and join you in America . . . I do not wish—I only hope."

Her birthday anniversaries had become something in the nature of a national holiday. The eightieth was the occasion for a round of celebrations lasting a week. On the eve of that day friends gathered about her and sang for her the negro spirituals she loved. A forest to be planted on the Hill of the Five was dedicated to her by the Women's International Zionist Organization. In the morning she spoke over the radio to the children of the country:

When I was young as you are who now are listening to my voice, the world existed without a telephone, without an automobile, without an airship, without a radio. Today, in my old age, when I have reached the years of strength, as the psalmist called the age of eighty, a marvellous invention grants me the possibility of sending my voice to thousands of little children, big boys and girls, and youth scattered to all corners of this land.

As you see, in the eighty years I have lived, many wonderful changes have taken place. But in one respect the world has not changed. Today, as long ago, good men and good women do noble acts; today, as long ago, wise men and wise women think great thoughts; today, as long ago, we, the Jewish people, still cherish the spirit and the ideals which have sustained us since the beginning of our nationhood. The soul does not change; it only learns to use new and better ways of communicating with other souls.

Because the world has not changed in these respects, youth and old age can meet, as I am privileged to meet you today with my voice and my soul; old age and youth can resolve together, as I should like you to resolve with me, to live nobly and wisely and energetically; and as Jews pledge ourselves, the young and the old together, to cherish and endeavor to realize our ideals as long as the breath of life is in us. This is my promise to you—this is the birthday gift I ask of you.

A dinner at the Hadassah Hospital on the mountaintop was followed by festivities at the Nurses Training School. "Towards midnight," wrote Dr. Magnes, "Miss Szold was in the middle of a hora which I did not see because by that time people with ordinary strength had long since left. Yesterday at the meeting she was full of pep and the old Nick . . . She is leaving this morning on another three days' tour of Youth Aliyah points."

As the invading armies drew near, friends repeatedly urged that she leave the country—the invaders would have scant respect for her four score years and two. Miss Szold would not yield to their entreaties. "What will they do to me? Make me scrub the streets?" Her head poked out of the window: "They need it!"

Henrietta Szold remained at her post, but her thoughts were turned longingly to the American scene, to the city of Baltimore, to years gone by and friends of long ago. To her sole surviving sister, Bertha, she wrote: "To think that my blue-eyed darling is a granny of three score and ten! And to think that I arranged my life—or that the war disarranged my life—so that I am not with her to celebrate it. It is a betrayal of the past . . . Fortunately you, in the companionship of your children and the seven grandchildren live in a throbbing present and in the hope of a quickened future. In thought I shall be with you on your day—and all my thoughts will be loving and longing."

Told of her sister's new home, she asks wistfully: "Is there a room for me, just a tiny one?"

In 1942 there appeared a book by Marvin Lowenthal, entitled, *Henrietta Szold: Life and Letters.* She had protested all along that she was not a fit subject for a biography; in thanking Mr. Lowenthal for the copy sent to her, she wrote that she held to her old opinion, to which he answered: "If I can imagine your going to Hell, which somehow I cannot, I know what you would say at the gate: 'Am I really worth wasting the coal on?' "

Not that she failed to enjoy her reading of the book, but it was a new phenomenon that required a period of mental adjustment, even as putting on a new dress required, for her, many preliminary inspections and adjustments: "I finally succeeded in making of myself a neutral, as it were, and I read and read and rushed through the book at one wild dash. So long as I could put outside of my consciousness that it was 'me', I must confess I read with pleasure, and certainly with admiration of Marvin Lowenthal's skill and taste."

In March, 1944, she suffered a severe attack of dysentery followed by gout. The suggestion that she go to the hospital met with flat rebellion. She couldn't work there, and she knew, besides, that there was a shortage of beds. Dr. Kleeberg didn't argue the point; he proceeded, instead, to enumerate the treatments she required—injections, medicines, special diet, nursing, three daily visits from her physician. Miss Szold looked at him. "I see. You want me to make it easier for you. You want me to say I will go to the hospital. May I work?"

Her hospital room faced the east. She sat occasionally on the balcony; the view was one she loved—the great drop to the Dead Sea, miles away, and beyond, the purple hills of Moab, eternally the same, eternally changing. Her vision had become impaired by slowly forming cataracts. "You don't know how it hurts me that I can't see it any more; describe it to me," she said to a fellow-patient. The twittering of the birds in the early hours was welcome to her: "We ought to have a little fountain in the garden so that the birds can come in from the desert and refresh themselves."

Some weeks later she was allowed to go home, but soon

became ill again. One day when there was a sudden change in the weather—storm and a furious blast of wind—she was seized by a chill. The attack, followed by fever, was a serious setback. Now even her four-minute walk to the office became difficult, and she had to take a taxi.

At the end of July came another attack of pneumonia. She went again to the hospital, then to the Nurses Home where two small rooms were prepared for her use. Through the good offices of Dr. Magnes and the cooperation of the British military, a stock of penicillin was flown from Egypt for her—she was the first civilian in Palestine to have the benefit of the new drug. On good days, when her physician asked her how she was feeling, she answered: "Let me think. I think my head aches, and my joints, and my fingers a little. Do you want my diagnosis? Age. If you have a medicine against age, give it to me; if not, let me alone."

The attending physician marvelled at the aged woman's youthful body—skin white, smooth, and firm, like that of a young woman; muscles good, and, except for the lines on the face, no wrinkle anywhere or other sign of age. Never had he seen a like phenomenon.

In talk with Mrs. Sulamith Cantor, Supervisor of Nurses, Miss Szold announced: "When I get well, I will permit nobody to come and lay burdens on me. I will do my work, only my work." "Very well, Miss Szold, I promise you that I will not come to bother you." "You! Oh, no, I don't mean you. Certainly you may come."

Her Youth Aliyah secretaries, Emma Ehrlich and Hans Beyth, conferred with her daily. She received the few visitors permitted—Dr. Magnes, Dr. Weizmann, Ira Hirschmann. Lord Gort, High Commissioner, announced that he was coming to visit the hospital, and expressed the wish to meet Henrietta Szold. Told that he was expected, she insisted on dressing and greeting him in the Great Hall below. "Lord Gort is a gentleman," some one interposed. "He will not object to climbing these stairs to meet you." She replied: "If he is gentleman enough to climb the stairs for me, I am lady enough to go down to greet him." She was on hand in the Great Hall when he arrived.

Dr. Magnes told of a visit to her. "The morning was sunny and her chair was tucked into the one shady corner of the balcony. After fifteen minutes or so of talk, which was very lively on her part, I suggested that it was too sunny and that, since the room was made up, we go in. I approached her, made a mock courteous bow, crooked my arm and said: "May I have this dance with you?" She took my arm, rose from her chair, and shook her finger at me: 'You think you are going to get out of this, do you? I shall show you.' She took both my hands and led me about in gentle circles, singing a German ditty . . . We could hardly get over the brightness of her whole being that sunny morning."

Though racked by pain, she still shared in her imagination the experiences of her loved ones overseas. She was relieved that her niece was about to be settled in her new home, while her husband, a Red Cross worker overseas, was with her on leave: "I am glad for his sake as well as hers. If he must again leave her, it is somewhat of a solace that he must tax his memory rather than stretch his imagination in order to have a picture of her new entourage. For which reason I am grateful to you for having described the arrangement of the rooms and the setting of Sarah's new home as you did. Nothing adds to the twinges of homesickness so much as change of locale."

She, alas, must stretch her imagination, and it carries her to the little garden and the two-year-old, Bertha's grandchild, who plays there: "I am sure she gambols in the garden at Mount Washington like the 'armes, armes Laemmchen' (poor little lamb) you were taught to read with becoming pathos. I leave the reason for pathos out in Martha's gamboling, and imagine only her fat little legs, moving nimbly about as my matchsticks cannot."

Her sleep was filled with dreams. "I have been dreaming a great deal, as I haven't dreamed since my youth. There is hardly a night in which I don't have some sort of contact with our mother. She isn't always the central figure of the dream, but she is there . . . It is a nightly experience, this dipping into the past. It is natural because my bed leisure, of which there is a great deal, is filled with pictures of the past. I don't dismiss them, because their place would be taken by vain worry over the work I am neglecting perforce."

She would not urge Bertha to come to her: "I need not tell you how much I long to see you. There hasn't been a day since you left me, in 1940, that I haven't cast up the chances of being reunited with you, but never at the expense of your seven grandchildren. After all, you too, like me, are not a young woman. The claims of your family upon you by far supersede mine . . . I write in direct language, without circumlocution. You will understand from my style that I feel strongly on the subject. I remember well how insistent your children were that you come back from Palestine before doors were closed. But not the memory of their urgence influences my attitude; it is my full acceptance of the rightness of their insistence. The same feeling ought to dominate them, and me along with them, to object to your undertaking the trip to me."

Problems—the world's and Palestine's—still engaged her mind. She asked for material on Basic English, in the hope that its principles could be applied to Hebrew in dealing with the mass immigration expected after the war. She speculated on that expected immigration. "I wonder," she wrote, "whether you could send me something that could put me on the track of wise planning. Don't say it's all a manner of means. It isn't—that is my experience. Or, I should say, the money will not be withheld if there is wisdom and strength of purpose."

Incidents in the last year of her life are taken with her accustomed zest. With ill-concealed glee she tells her sister in America, after carefully explaining the term "pin-up girl," that she, Henrietta, is the pin-up of some soldiers in the Jewish Brigade. She is delighted that her hair, which had been falling out as a result of her illness, is responding to treatment: "They say it is coming back. I hope so. I do not want to be a bald-headed old hag." (It came back the brown of her youth.) She rebels at her inactivity: "It appears I am 'contrary'—I don't want sympathy, and thought, and care, and consideration. I want to work!"

Shortly before her March illness Miss Szold learned that Boston University wished to confer on her the degree of Doctor of Humanities. The honor moved her deeply, particularly "being permitted in these days of many men's inhumanity to man to bear the title of Doctor of Humanities."

It was 3 A.M. in Jerusalem when, surrounded by friends, she took the citation. The room with its set-up of radio machinery seemed to her like a medieval magician's haunt, and all the eager listeners in it under the spell of necromancy. She felt this to be the greatest honor ever bestowed upon her.

On her last Yom Kippur (Day of Atonement) she read her prayers in bed. A letter to Bertha paid tribute to her nurse, a Youth Aliyah girl who had lost mother, father and three brothers in the Hitler carnage: "Yesterday she and my night nurse were graduated from the Nurses Training School, the twenty-fourth class to be sent out by Hadassah. As a rule, you may remember, I confer the diplomas on the graduates. This year, of all years, the year in which I have had such outstanding opportunity to judge the value of the training . . . I had to content myself with a written greeting which was read out by Dr. Magnes. The authorities tried to compensate me by arranging to have the procession of the nurses defile past the porch on which I spend my afternoons. It was a charming sight."

Last letter of all, November 26, 1944: "I want to add that there is no cause for worry about me. I feel that I am improving." Then growing weakness, and long periods of semi-consciousness, calling to her beloved Betsy across the seas.

One more satisfaction was granted her. Two leaders of Jewry stood at her bedside—Magnes and Weizmann—whose opposing views on Jewish state versus bi-national state had kept them irreconcilably apart. Their hands were clasped together, both over hers, and in that handclasp her eyes saw present comfort and future promise. On the evening of Tuesday, February 13, 1945, she fell into her last sleep.

20. *Self-Portrait*

" 'The earth abideth forever' "

SOME QUALITY in Henrietta Szold, usually called modesty, made it difficult for her to regard herself as in any way exceptional. She tried to see herself objectively, to make an impersonal personal appraisal of her qualities, and in self-appraisal she acknowledged certain points of superiority. These were: first, a physical constitution that permitted her a much longer than normal working day; second, a flair for organization including a gift for detail; third, an exacting conscience. To these three qualities she sometimes added a fourth—a pretty big capacity for righteous indignation.

For the homage paid her she always tried to find explanations. Of her visit to Berlin in 1935, she told her sisters: "I cannot hide from you that what happened to me here kept me in a state of bewildered wonderment. I have been trying to analyze why the routine administrative work I did should have impressed the German Jewish community so deeply. I have reached a conclusion: it is all a matter of language. My mastery of the German language brought me near to them and them to me . . . The exaggerated praise is ascribable to the excited state of Jewish feeling in Germany. But you had a right to know what happened to me. I had to write about myself."

Another time: "Somehow or other I am a humbug. I seem to have won golden opinions which I have not earned. I am not what I seem to others. I have told you this in other language before."

In 1918, when placed in charge of the newly-organized Department of Education of the Zionist Organization of America, she wrote: "This work was thrust upon me at twenty-four hours' notice. I spent the twenty-four hours in vain protest. I feel myself thoroughly unfitted for it. I haven't the physical strength for it . . . So far as the journalistic part of it goes, I have a perfect aversion to it. I have never taken to journalism. I acknowledge its supreme value, but I have no affinity for it . . . This new work involves adjustment with established agencies that have been independent of each other. However, I am not finding it difficult to deal with them, not because I am particularly tactful or diplomatic—on the contrary, because I am only truthful. I lay my cards on the table in all these cases, and I warn them that, so far as I am concerned, I am not fencing with words."

In 1921: "Coming to Palestine has not changed my fate. I still stand about, as it were, waiting for things to come along to be done. I haven't long to wait. They come in shoals and my days are as disunified as ever and as crowded . . . I see now that by some hocus-pocus of which I am guilty, though not consciously a sinner—some trick of manner, perhaps, rather than sterling quality—I kept the [American Zionist Medical] Unit quiet all summer."

One hint there is that she herself recognized that she possessed some inner source of strength and intuitive wisdom: "Perhaps I overrate myself in what I am going to say now . . . I find that, old as I am, in a certain sense I have not stopped growing. While I don't understand, while my intellect is an organ of narrow limitations, my inner world—perhaps it is my world of feeling, of instinct—expands."

She could not overcome her aversion to personal publicity—she belonged to the days when to men and women of breeding the uses of publicity were not sweet, but closely allied to vulgarity. After reading reports of a meeting at which her name had been given what she considered undue prominence, she wrote: "I feel the unseemliness of it all the way across the seas. You remember how we used to deprecate the adulation paid to Mr. Brandeis... In my case there is no excuse for it—not even the excuse of eminent ability . . . I need not confess to you I love love—that I crave it with human naturalness. But it must manifest itself in confidence, not in words."

Of Madame Curie: "Here was a woman who *really* deserved homage! Here was a woman who had given something to the world. And yet, how private her life had been. How she avoided publicity and applause."

When a group of young girls wrote to say they would like to call their society by her name, it was with some reluctance that she granted permission. Only those whose lives had been completed, she told them, should be so honored, because the value of their work could then be read like a book. A living person was a fragment out of a book. To one group which assured her they would try to be a credit to her name, she replied: "And what would happen if in the days left to me I should be something that would not be a credit to the fine young girls who are uniting for a public purpose?"

Friends pleaded with Miss Szold to write the story of her life, only to be put off with one or another vague or unsatisfactory answer. At times she declared that her life lacked the elements of drama that made for good reading. Or she would assert that she was not a writer. Of this let the reader judge. The following is an excerpt from an article written on shipboard.

There is on board one who might have been a leader of Palestinians, one who has attained distinction and title, a man of fine presence, with a noble thinker's brow. He chose otherwise. He chose to become *Acher*.* I heard him say that he had had an idea of visiting Palestine, but he had heard that traveling in Palestine was hard. So he desisted. He decided to stay in Egypt. Traveling in Palestine too hard? Yes, for the Jew who has found traveling through life on Jewish roads too hard, and is driven to self-annihilation by means of a few drops of water. What passed through his mind when Professor Kellner spoke of his son in Benjamina, and of his hopes, which are a nation's hopes? What inconvenient memories stirred when his eyes fell upon the Hebrew characters in the books lying all around? When the sounds of Hebrew song and conversation fell upon his ears? Did he call himself *Acher* as he looked out upon the blue sea? Did thoughts of self-annihilation in water again cross his mind? Not drops of water, but deeps of water, drowning memory itself? The brow, the keen eye, revealed nothing more than his mouth had spoken; he had decided to remain behind in Egypt, where traveling is as easy now as the fleshpots were alluring in other times.

Or is the following to be understood as self-justification for her refusal? It is excerpted from the Introduction Miss Szold wrote for Rebekah Kohut's *My Portion*.

Jewish literature is singularly wanting in personal reminiscences . . . That Jewish literature should be deficient in personal material lay in the nature of Jewish life as it was perforce constituted. In the over-

* Acher—literally *other*. Used here to mean apostate.

whelming sum of Jewish communal woe and communal aspiration, the individual sank out of sight. His personal desires, trials and successes were frail straws rapidly swirled out of sight on the stream of community life. From the Jewish point of view the public weal was better served by reticence than by self-expression. In the moving Jewish drama, the chorus alone was vocal. Only at critical times it would happen that the recluse scholar disengaged himself from the background as a speaking character, to admonish in the face of spiritual backsliding or encourage in the face of danger; or the man of affairs was forced into leadership, to save his brethren by his wealth or his resourceful wit, when expulsion or massacre threatened. These two outstanding figures were not tempted to self-revelation. The scholar's work spoke for him; the intercessor's was too delicate to court publicity. They remained silent, and by their silence emphasized the relation of the individual to the community, and of the community to the individual.

An attempt to keep a diary after her arrival in Palestine in 1920 had to be given up; life made too many demands upon her to grant even that little leisure.

In the orderliness of Miss Szold's working habits no unsightly papers or stray material appeared on desk or in drawers. But in the corner of a drawer odds and ends found after her death left their own silent record. Among them were the sonnet, *High Flight,* by John C. Magee, Jr., killed in action at nineteen; the lines by Emma

Lazarus, engraved on the base of the Statue of Liberty in New York Harbor:

> "....... Give me your tired, your poor,
> Your huddled masses yearning to breathe free,
> The wretched refuse of your teeming shore,
> Send these, the homeless, tempest-tost, to me,
> I lift my lamp beside the golden door!"

a passage from *The Wind in the Willows,* by Kenneth C. Grahame, one of her favorite books; Elizabeth Barrett Browning's *The Cry of the Children,* beginning

> "Do ye hear the children weeping, O my brothers,
> Ere the sorrow comes with years?"

and

> "I shall pass through this world but once.
> Any good thing, therefore, that I can do,
> Any kindness I can show to any human being,
> Let me do it now.
> Let me not defer it nor neglect it,
> For I shall not pass this way again."

Is it out of place to mention that along with these was a newspaper clipping giving directions for reducing waist and stomach muscles?

In her observations and reflections upon those she admired, she often seems, involuntarily, to portray herself.

Of Aaron Aaronsohn, upon his tragic death in 1919,* she wrote:

* Aaron Aaronsohn was lost from a British government plane in a flight over the Channel at a time when he was believed to be carrying documents granting the Jews in Palestine important political concessions. A report gained currency that the plane's pilot was seen in Paris after Aaronsohn's disappearance.

> Aaronsohn was a seer of visions. A seer of visions, not a dreamer. He was too energetic in mind and body to be a dreamer. He was active, not passive; never borne down by lassitude; never acquiescent, always constructive . . . A seer of constructive visions . . . Everything fed the central aim that pervaded every nook and corner of his mind . . . He lived as many lives as he knew languages, and yet he lived but one unified life. The foreign psychology never overlaid his own. His own he maintained in its peculiar strength no matter what he brought to it from the outside. Knowledge, because he assimilated it, did not diminish his originality; copious and diversified reading did not stifle it; contact with all sorts and conditions of men gave it elasticity . . . What came from the outside was fuel. The fire it fed was his immutable vision.

Theodor Herzl died in 1904. In the August *Maccabaean* Henrietta Szold wrote:

> Herzl's greatest trait was not the charm of his personality, the royal dignity of his presence, his capacity for devotion, his gift of harmonizing opposite views and parties, his statesman's insight and comprehensive outlook. Greater and rarer than all these was the subordination of his personality to the idea. His inner world developed with the idea he fought for. That he with his non-Jewish education and environment should have conceived the idea of political Zionism was a flash of inspiration . . . That he grew Jewish, engaged the support of Jewish Jews, modified his first plan in obedience to the centuries-old Jewish ideal, learnt day by day to read life and its problems in Hebrew fashion—therein lies his genius and our

comfort . . . His ideal grew, he grew with it, and as they grew together, the means of realizing the ideal took on larger dimensions, deeper fervor, spiritual force. This he taught us—and the lesson is our consolation—"one generation passeth away, and another generation cometh"—but the cause, the idea, abideth forever.

Of Nathan Straus: "To me it seems that Nathan Straus, always thought of with his wife at his side, is the man of faith. Faith is the key to his being and his doing . . . Faith looks forward . . . Faith makes bold . . . The man of faith does not shrink from the task of moving mountains . . . The man who identifies himself with youth and its care is a man of faith! . . . And because he was a man of faith he espoused the cause of Zionism."

It was not only the great and the near great who called forth her passionate encomiums. Rose Kaplan* entered Hadassah's service as a nurse in 1913. Four years later she was dead in Alexandria. Of her Henrietta Szold wrote: "An unalterable record lies before us . . . It is a noble record, and it has the simplicity characteristic of heroism and of truth. No matter what their contents are in detail, all the pages of her life bear the same heading: Service to suffering humanity . . . To shirk a duty was a deadly sin; to perform it half-heartedly an unpardonable crime . . . Rose Kaplan teaches us that one can be a soldier of peace and can do one's work amid peaceful surroundings and yet with an exaltation of spirit that raises one above the crowd . . . The earth must be beautified. It must be a temple for the human soul, for the human body. It must be a habitation worthy of man, created in the image of his creator. And were you to have asked her how should

* See page 52.

the earth be made such a habitation, she would have had a simple answer: by shifting the center of gravity from the individual to the community. Only in the youth of man may the center of gravity be the individual. Once the individual is educated, he must merge his individuality into the community and offer it endless public service. That would have been her answer."

At Henrietta Szold's graveside there was no eulogy spoken. This was in deference to her wishes. Her eulogies were the tears of the thousands who trudged up the rocky slope after her body, and of the other thousands who, because she so wished it, stayed, heavy-hearted, at their daily tasks. But perhaps here, too, we can find words of her own which might now have been spoken about her. She had spoken them of the lost leaders, Louis D. Brandeis and Menahem Ussischkin, both of whom died in the fall of 1941. She spoke of the lament which had arisen, the feeling of forlornness which had come over Jewry for leaders whose places could not be filled:

"Such mourners seem to me to fail to understand that the pessimist Koheleth who tells us that one generation passeth away and another generation cometh, must have been an optimist, for he ends his sentence with the conclusion that the earth abideth forever. They who refuse to draw strength from his conclusion are of little faith, and they lack full appreciation of the leaders we have had to lose. Because Brandeis and Ussischkin lived and worked among us, leaders will continue to exist, rising from the masses or from the recesses from which Herzl and Brandeis emerged. Leadership will not be lacking. That is the meaning to me of their work, their faith, their vision, their leadership. This audience is the witness."

21. *Love—Work—Order*

HUMBUG," Henrietta was apt to call herself, this gentlewoman of Baltimore, partly in defense against the adulation poured out on her, partly to indicate what she felt to be gaps in her education, particularly in her preparation for the specific tasks which, one after another, became her responsibility. Destined seemingly for a life of serene scholarship, neither she nor any one could have guessed the paths she was to tread. Over and over in her later years came the astonished exclamation: "Why am I doing this!" as again and again she took formlessness, chaos, into her hands, shaped it into form and body, and with creative artistry breathed into it life and spiritual meaning.

The mind of Henrietta Szold was governed by no preconceptions; it yielded its integrity to no party line even though dictated by the organizations to which she gave a lifetime of loyal service. Doctrinairism never took the place of independent thinking. Coupled with her intellectual and moral independence were a flexibility and a youthfulness which enabled her to adjust easily and quickly to changing situations, to work with whatever means came to hand, and with all sorts and conditions of men, women and children.

College training for women, later to become a commonplace, was for few of her generation, but the intellectual discipline to which she subjected herself surpassed by far what any average college training of today would offer. "It is because of you, Henrietta Szold, that I am here," Mayor Fiorello La Guardia said to her when he received her on the steps of New York's City Hall and presented her with the key to the city. He was referring to the part Miss Szold had taken in building up a system of night schools* to which countless immigrants owed whatever success they achieved in their American careers.

Her vision and initiative brought into being, in turn, a national organization of Zionist women which now counts 300,000 members; a hospital system, the first of its kind in the Middle East; a complete and integrated complex of child welfare institutions ranging from prenatal to post-natal clinics, pre-school care, and school hygiene; a system of school luncheons; playgrounds; a Nurses' Training School; a social service program and training school for social workers; an organization for mass youth immigration, the Youth Aliyah; finally, at the end of her life, the Child and Youth Welfare Foundation. In all her undertakings this "humbug" so mastered their technical and administrative aspects that the experts came to her for counsel.

Years before most of these developments took place Miss Szold wrote from Palestine: "My sisters used to call me 'stick-in-the-mud' because I was 'set' in my ways, loath to change my habits. I was homekeeping like a cat. I think even they—sisters are proverbially hard critics—would concede my adaptability if they saw me adjust myself to new work and new conditions." For this home-loving woman, at fifty-nine, had left her homeland, given up her comforting surroundings and the companionship of friends and family, and transported herself to an old-new land—a land of Arabs and of Jews—the Arabs living in

* See Chapter 3.

the primitive pastoral setting of a feudal civilization, the Jewish element harking back to medieval centuries, yet containing within itself the makings of a brave new world.

One of the adjustments Miss Szold said frequently that she found difficult to make was the adjustment to a new language. Although Hebrew was familiar to her through the pages of Bible and prayer book, it could be baffling when used in daily speech. She was well able to express herself adequately (those qualified to judge stressed the fact that never once had they heard a mistake in her Hebrew speech), but it was many years before she lost a certain sense of inarticulateness in using the language. Her own exquisite sense of color and nuance in words could accept no slightest derogation from the vigor, completeness and ease so fully at her command in English and in German.

Seeing her bundled in sweaters, shivering in the bitter Jerusalem winter over an inadequate brazier or equally inadequate oil stove, working her pen with frozen fingers and swathing herself for bed in layer upon layer of woolen clothing, or scrambling donkey-back up the steep slopes of Safed, the flexibility of her life matching the flexibility and resilience of her mind, no one could have guessed that anything in her life had ever been "set."

From first to last, in all her ministrations, there was nothing impersonal, detached, or aloof. In one of his letters Keats wrote that when he saw a bird pecking on the lawn, he was, for the time being, that bird. As complete as that was her consciousness of the human being before her. Yvonne Leonard wrote in *The Palestine Tribune* a few weeks after Miss Szold's death:

> A few years ago, newly arrived in Palestine, I came to a communal settlement with a whole lot of refugees. I was very raw; about two hours had passed

of the two years needed to become a Palestinian. I felt horrible. Nobody seemed able to speak my language. So I sat down on my bed and took a framed picture of my mother out of my suitcase. My mother I had had to leave behind in the hell of Europe.

I tried to make people understand that I wanted a nail to hang mother's picture on the wall. But nobody saw how urgent this was; there were so many more important things to attend to.

Still I could not see any, and started crying. At this point an elderly lady asked me in a language I could understand why I was so desperately unhappy.

"I want a nail, I want to nail mother's picture on the wall," I answered.

"Just a minute," said the lady, and returned a few moments later with a nail and hammer and started to bang furiously at the wall. When I looked up mother's picture was hanging in its place and the lady had gone.

Years later, my papers and myself quite in order and the initial refugee unhappiness long forgotten, friends asked me to attend an official social evening at the Ahava near Haifa. Miss Szold was to be there, as well as a few other people of interest. I went, and after a while was asked to come to Miss Szold as she would like to speak to me. I was surprised, and thought it must be a misunderstanding. Still, over I went and introduced myself. "O yes, I know your name," she replied. "What I wanted to know is, are you getting your nails now when you need them?"

The multiplicity of the calls upon her time for needs real or imagined, claims justified and unjustified, never dulled the keen edge of her awareness. Conferences were given without stint on purely personal problems, and services were voluntarily rendered in countless ways to acquaintance and stranger. Well-meaning friends protested in vain against the sapping of her strength. To one she replied: "If I refuse to receive him, even though I know in my heart that I can do nothing, he will always think that if he could have talked to me, things might have turned out differently for him. That satisfaction at least of permitting him to put his case before me, I must give him."

Never did a visitor receive in Miss Szold's presence a feeling that time was pressing, or that other problems were on her mind than those of the caller. Her attention was as uncluttered as the desk at which she sat, and her mind's quiet could not but bring a feeling of quiet to her visitor. In the unhurried walk to the office, she took time to note the twitter of the birds and the signs of coming spring, to stoop and comfort a sick dog.

The satisfaction and rewards that came to her were many. As early as her first year in Palestine, in the midst of problems and difficulties, she wrote in triumph: "And for the first time I saw one of my hopes connected with Zionism realized . . . I faced a human problem in which Jews are concerned, and alone concerned, and I forgot wholly that they are Jews. And so did they."

Although she never lost her longing for the deep woods of her native Maryland, she responded joyously to the poetry in the Palestine landscape—the soft, clear air, the abundant spring flora, the "insistent" rocks reflecting in their bareness every light and shade of the changing summer sky, the flight of storks northward, punctuated by their periodic circlings. "The land is treeless, largely waterless; at this season the green has largely disappeared, and the dry thornbushes almost crackle under the hot sun—and yet it is beautiful, so beautiful that I almost resent our intention to make it blossom and bear fruit. The stones are soft with colorfulness, and between them spring up blossoms so curiously adapted to the peculiarity of the land that one cannot wonder enough."

Love and devotion were showered on her; eulogies left her embarrassed and wincing; after one of them she cried out: "Today I attended another of my funerals!" Honorary degrees* were bestowed upon her by the Jewish Institute of Religion and by Dropsie College, as well as by Boston University. She was named one of the ten greatest contemporary women by John Haynes Holmes. On which she commented: "Silly! to be explained only by the fact that Mr. Holmes has only the slightest knowledge of me, derived from three or four casual conversations." The Palestine Government, notoriously antipathetic to Jewish interests, once informed Henrietta Szold that she need only make her wishes known to have them granted. When asked why she did not avail herself of the offer, she answered: "They know well enough that I'm not likely to take advantage of it. That's why they made the offer."

Scrupulous about the use of public funds, Miss Szold rarely indulged in any but second-class travel (third, when second was not available) except on a few occasions when travel accommodations were "arranged" for her behind her back. "It is wicked luxury," she wrote then. "Even on the *Esperia* it was not necessary, but here it is voluptuousness." On the Palestine roads her travel was by bus and third-class rail, unless a taxi was indispensable. "I am no more than one of the people of Israel," she said, when found waiting for a bus on a windy corner. Dr. Rubinow

* In 1950 the International Union for the Protection of the Child awarded its Medal of Honor posthumously to Henrietta Szold and to Hans Beyth.

earned a scolding for ordering a rug to protect her feet from the cold stone floor of the office. Nor, sitting wrapped in a shawl, shivering, would she order a stove brought in for herself; the others were without stoves—why should she be an exception? Taxi bills came under careful scrutiny. "How much is the bill?" she inquired of one driver. "The time was four hours; the bill comes to so-and-so much." "Oh no, it was three and three-quarter hours—that is twelve piastres less, and you will not get any more. I am paying you out of public funds." When she traveled in Europe, on various missions, hours were spent translating currencies, charging fractions of pounds, dollars, francs, marks, in proper allotments of traveling expenses to this, that, and the other body.

At the hotel where she lived for years a tablemate could not help noticing that invariably she chose the least expensive foods. Later the reason was divulged—not by her. She wished to help, so far as she was able, in keeping down the expenses of the hotel proprietor who was in financial difficulties.

Henrietta Szold had one faculty which to the layman seems almost miraculous—a power of complete cooperation between the conscious and subconscious mind. Professor Bentwich told of her falling off to sleep at night while he was reading a manuscript aloud to her. Her eyes closed, her breath came in the regular rhythm of the sleeper; to all appearance she was sound asleep. But when something in the text showed inaccuracy, her mind reacted at once: "No, that is not correct. It should be thus and so." Her secretaries commented on the same phenomenon. One of them, assured she was asleep, skipped a few lines in her reading. "Go back; read it all," came the order. At a social workers' conference which she was attending after a full day's work, she gave the impression of being in a deep sleep, but when the conference ended, she summed up the discussion, with no notes to help her, making apt comments on the evening's deliberations.

Hans Beyth and others told of a trip taking them through the Youth Aliyah settlements in the Emek. She dozed off in the car. Five minutes before arriving at the first stop, she awoke, turned to Beyth, and began reviewing the list of problems to be discussed. As they rode on after the first visit, she fell asleep again, and again awoke five minutes before reaching the next stop. So it went all along the Emek, from one stopping point to the next, the "alarm clock" within her functioning with perfect timing to her needs. A state of self-controlled hypnosis, the psychologist calls it.

To her home, on the Sabbath, as to a shrine, came people of all sorts—a journalist from America, a scientist from the University, a German rabbi, a group of children on a visit to Jerusalem, a pupil nurse from the Training School, tourists with or without introduction, friends and neighbors and, during the war, soldiers from the front. She always managed to create a common atmosphere, to make the humblest visitor feel easy and welcome. Each one "belonged." Dr. Ernst Simon, Professor of Education at the Hebrew University, told of having been in her room one Sabbath when two youngsters knocked timidly at her door, entered, and said: "Please excuse us; we have come to Jerusalem to see the Wailing Wall and Miss Szold." "Indeed," he continued, "the children did come to see her because of her illustrious name; but when they departed, they did not depart as men taking leave of holy stones. They will remember forever the delightful and lively conversation they had with this old-young lady."

With the young people who came from Germany before the war she had at once found common ground through her intimate knowledge of German classic literature. Later she established the same rapport with the boys of the Oriental communities, who had no literary background. When one of the leaders asked how she did it, her only explanation was: "At my age, youth is youth."

One normal gift had passed her by—she could not sing a note. At seventy, pledging her teacher* to secrecy, she began a series of lessons in singing. She had to prove to herself that she could at least master the scale—she who delighted in song could not go to her grave without that accomplishment. For six months she took singing lessons—and did master the scale. It was one of her triumphs.

Her sense of smell was extraordinarily acute. On a walk through the streets of Baltimore, Adele saw her nostrils twitch violently. "What's the matter?" asked Adele. Henrietta sniffed the air. "Adele, I smell a paulownia imperialis!" "Where? I don't see one." "But I smell one," insisted Henrietta. They walked a block and turned the corner. The younger sister still did not catch the voluptuous aroma, but there down the street stood the tree with its rich, purple, orchid-like blooms.

On the road between Ludd and Ramleh stands an ancient sycamore which she liked to visit, even at the cost of a detour. "Wait, I'll show you one of my treasures," she would say to her companion on the trip. "There are few trees like this in the country." When she passed newly-forested land she took note of how the trees had grown since she last saw them. And to the lady who protested that she didn't have to know the name or family of a beautiful flower in order to enjoy it, the rejoinder came: "I don't understand. If you meet an attractive man and are inter-

* Louise Zeitlin who settled in Jerusalem after a career on the concert stage in England and the Dominions.

ested in him, don't you want to be introduced to him, to know his name, and something of his background?"

The phenomenon of anti-Semitism baffled her. The Russian persecutions and pogroms of the 80's and 90's could be explained on the ground that Russia was still a country living in the mists of feudalism. But it was not so easy to account for German anti-Semitism of the late nineteenth century, which was fostered by the preacher of the Imperial Court and led to wild rioting. For was not Germany the home of an advanced and advancing civilization? Yet, even as early as 1881, she had written on the basis of her own observation:

"The German of the lower classes, still more the Austrian, is so eager to avail himself of pleasures and amusements that he often shirks duties of the most sacred kind. These pleasures, instead of refining him, as their character might lead us to expect, bestialize him."

To one friend she confided the belief that anti-Semitism could not be eradicated because of the annual recounting of the Crucifixion story. "It will go on forever without loss of potency," she said. Her own first personal encounter with anti-Semitism came on her first trip to Europe. She had formed a pleasant shipboard companionship with a family of culture and refinement: it was broken off abruptly—she was Jewish! "It cut through the friendship like a knife."

There was no answering vindictiveness in her: she was singularly free from the feeling itself and from the sense of oppression it brings. Hearing a young woman, newly arrived from a European hell-hole, explode: "If only I could spit at one German Nazi!" Miss Szold looked at her incredulously. "No, would you really?" and proceeded to quiet the girl with reminders of the great German philosophers and poets. The most regrettable effect on the Jewish community of the Arab outbreak of 1929 was, she felt, that the hatred of the attackers engendered an answering hatred. For that she was truly sorry.

Part of the soul-trouble of the Jew, Miss Szold felt, was his bitterness about the lack of understanding, the indifference, of his Christian neighbors. She took every occasion possible to combat that tendency. Acknowledging a contribution to Youth Aliyah, made by a Christian donor in Baltimore, she wrote: "It is comforting to have such acts brought to one's attention . . . I am convinced that the Miss Mackubins of the world are not so rare as we Jews often complain. Our Jewish extremity has brought to light many acts expressing indignation at the Hitler policy—in our case indignation is more than sympathy . . . I value those protestors who, like Niebuhr in America and many like him all over the world, not omitting Germany itself, have spoken out valiantly and forcefully." Conversely she hoped that always, when speaking of the catastrophe that had overtaken the Jews, mention would be made of the fellow-sufferers—the Catholics, the Protestants, the socialists, the labor men.

But action—that was another matter. No one person could do more than fight a tiny bit of the world problem. For Henrietta Szold, that bit was the Jewish problem. In his appraisal of Miss Szold's impress on American life, Dr. Rubinow took note of her attitude: "She could have made an even greater [impress] were it not for two factors —first, her amazing self-effacement, and secondly, her absorbing preoccupation with Jewish life."

Of all who spoke of her there was only one who spoke in disappointment. She had failed, she said, to find in Henrietta Szold the delight that others had found: it was one of her great regrets. A few of those questioned mentioned one point of weakness—an occasional error of judgment, in spite of her usually acute perception of character and intelligence—which led to mistakes in filling important posts. Sometimes the error was ascribable to her inordinate respect for professional training; sometimes, it must be admitted, she failed to see through the flattery of a sycophant. In either case, once she had completely and wholeheartedly accepted a person, her critical faculties were put to sleep. One lady, refusing to make any adverse comment, quoted a European proverb: "Even the sun has flecks."

As one reads the words written of Henrietta Szold by men and women of balanced judgment whose daily lives ran along with hers, one cannot but be struck by the frequent use of the term "prophet." Dr. Samuel Spiro, supervising physician of the Youth Aliyah, felt the magic of her personality. "There are those," he said, "with illustrious names, whose luster fades when one comes into close contact with them. The reverse was true in the case of Henrietta Szold. The closer one came within the range of her personality the greater became the wonder at her being and her achievement." Dr. Spiro wrote after Miss Szold's death: but even during her lifetime the same note was struck.

From Dr. Friedenwald, writing of the accomplishments of the Hadassah Medical Organization: "Little could I imagine what the next quarter of a century would bring forth. Little could I dream of the power and the ability and the vision of Hadassah to create and to bring to successful achievement its vast agencies. Had any of the officers given expression to such views, she would have been regarded as a megalomaniac. And yet I suspect that there was one person who looked into the future with the eyes of a prophet—Henrietta Szold."

Alice Seligsberg declared: "I have long held a belief that may be regarded as mystic though I think it is based on evidence; the belief that the gift of foreknowledge, of prophetic vision around the circumference of human action . . . is granted only to persons of great virtue, great purity of purpose, great consecration. In my opinion, this is what the founder of Hadassah possesses; that is why we have developed according to the first plans laid in the early years by Henrietta Szold."

From Mrs. Alexander Marx, another close friend: "It always struck me that in the current English translations of the Bible we find the word *massa,* which is frequently used when a prophet has a certain mission assigned to him, translated by 'burden'. Thus we often read 'burden of the word of the Lord,' as if all true vision weighs on men like a burden until it is transformed into action . . . The word 'burden' has become entwined in the pattern of Miss Szold's life."

From Dorothy Kahn, newspaper correspondent: "To describe the response of the people of the countryside . . . is not easy. To witness it is a deeply touching experience, of which one can say very little. She walks among the simple people, the nearest approach to a prophet that modern Palestine has seen. Schoolchildren wait shyly at gates with bunches of roses; housewives offer apple strudel baked with the first apples. No problem of theirs is too large or too small for her. She discusses with them. She laughs with them. She cries with them. And she scolds them. She is of them, and yet her visits are in the nature of a triumphal procession."

After her death, the Flatbush Ministers' Association, a Protestant organization, passed a resolution offering sympathy to its Jewish friends and acclaiming Henrietta Szold a "true prophetess" in Israel. "These words of mine," explained the Reverend Karl M. Chworodsky, who had introduced the resolution, "simply recorded my conviction that Henrietta Szold belongs in the prophetic tradition of the great souls of Israel."

Henrietta Szold's vision was tied to place, not to time. She could envisage failure for the hour and the day, even for the century—complete and devastating failure. "Unless we have patience," she warned at one time, "we will destroy the work of our own hands." Frequently pessimistic concerning the immediate outlook, she never faltered in work, never took hand from the plough, looked always to the "saving remnant." "Be the present what it may," she said in one time of political trouble, "we are an eternal people. We shall 'return' from this captivity with our inheritance undiminished. It is not for me to say how and when, but I believe it is right and proper for each one of us to proclaim the faith that lives in him. That is the antidote to discouragement and despair; it is the life-giving tonic by which a people maintains its eternal, incorruptible values."

The sweep of her vision—backwards to the dawn of her people's history, forward to eternity—enabled her to look upon destruction itself, and without faltering to find words of strength to clothe her forward-looking thoughts. "We have been forgetting, or at least not reminding ourselves frequently enough, that Zionism is more inclusive even than Palestine. The upbuilding of Palestine is an incorporation of the Zionist idea, but not the incorporation of the whole of it . . . Zionism is more than Palestinianism. To know and feel that will be a source of consolation if might should prove greater than right, and a source of strength if our practical work should have to be intermitted or its rate retarded. To know and feel it may become the salvation of Jewish Palestine itself, as it is the salvation of the Diaspora."

In the one hand, denunciation for wrong: in the other, solace and hope. What but the pattern of the prophets!

It would be unfair to the memory of Henrietta Szold to portray her as an angel: she was too well-rounded an individual for that. Some friends, startled to hear a vigorous pounding from her conference room, queried her later. "Oh," came the bland explanation, "I just wanted to show them what I could do." Her bursts of anger were not always a pretense; they were genuine and prodigious. But once the storm was over, it was completely over—no ranklings and left-overs to be pawed at again and again. Though she could hardly be called a gourmet, she relished to the full a tasty meal, and anticipated with zest her visits to the Tel Aviv pension where the dishes most closely resembled the delicious cookery of her Hungarian mother. She could be irked by a gift of chocolate peppermints—that was the candy for old ladies, she said—although her favorite sweet was chocolate peppermint. No one could charge Henrietta Szold with personal vanity, yet she could draw attention to her dainty ankle and took a pardonable pride in the soft hair to which she gave one hundred brush strokes, later five hundred, every day.

The importance of the beauty parlor to her women friends was something of a mystery, but the day came when the mystery had to be fathomed, and Henrietta marched off to a clandestine appointment and demanded "the works." Everything went smoothly until the moment the lipstick was to be applied. Then she clapped her hands over her mouth: "I've got to draw the line somewhere."

And to hear Miss Szold tell a story, herself sometimes the butt, was a treat. Her friends still grow hilarious recalling the stories and her telling of them, and for her nieces and nephews the most vivid recollection of her visits is the recollection of laughter.

The sense of wonder at her never failed. Yet, however one tries, it remains impossible, as it always must with greatness, to fathom or define her quality. This story, that incident, a word or phrase here and there, lights her up, and for a moment there is a glimpse, but the essence continues to elude. Charm, wit, character, a mind both brilliant and profound—these are qualities possessed in some degree by many. Henrietta Szold had them all—and something more, besides. Was it perhaps that no word of hers, spoken or written, was ever a perfunctory word, no relationship ever a casual one? The elevator boy who generally carried her up to her friend's apartment was disappointed if he found she had gone up in his absence. To a middle-aged man who called on her in Palestine she spoke of the pleasure he had given her, a quarter of a century earlier, by his excellent bar-mitzvah reading. A cantor whose Hebrew diction she had commended cherished the compliment until his dying day. The rabbi's wife knew, without turning her head, when Miss Szold was in the synagogue, for then her husband's eyes turned automatically in the direction of that seat. And an Irish traffic cop in New York, one of her escort when she was received at City Hall, neglected to write out a ticket for a speeding motorist because that motorist bore the name of Szold.

Each one whose life crossed hers felt her his personal pride and joy. Few came within the sound of her voice but sensed enlargement and enrichment. Her memory will be a lasting heritage. Increasingly as the years go by her stature will be seen in its true proportions, and generations that did not touch her hand will feel the grace of her presence and call her blessed.

Addenda

New York, September 16, 1916

To Haym Peretz:

It is impossible for me to find words in which to tell you how deeply I was touched by your offer to act as "Kaddish" for my dear mother. I cannot even thank you—it is something that goes beyond thanks. It is beautiful, what you have offered to do—I shall never forget it.

You will wonder, then, that I cannot accept your offer. Perhaps it would be best for me not to try to explain to you in writing, but to wait until I see you to tell you why it is so. I know well, and appreciate what you say about, the Jewish custom; and Jewish custom is very dear and sacred to me. And yet I cannot ask you to say *Kaddish* after my mother. The Kaddish means to me that the survivor publicly and markedly manifests his wish and intention to assume the relation to the Jewish community which his parent had, and that so the chain of tradition remains unbroken from generation to generation, each adding its own link. You can do that for the generations of your family. I must do that for the generation of my family.

I believe that the elimination of women from such duties was never intended by our law and custom—women were freed from positive duties when they could not perform them, but not when they could. It was never intended that, if they could perform them, their performance of them should not be considered as valuable and valid as when one of the male sex performed them. And of the *Kaddish* I feel sure this is particularly true.

My mother had eight daughters and no son; and yet never did I hear a word of regret pass the lips of either my mother or my father that one of us was not a son. When my father died, my mother would not permit others to take her daughters' place in saying the *Kaddish,* and so I am sure I am acting in her spirit when I am moved to decline your offer. But beautiful your offer remains nevertheless, and, I repeat, I know full well that it is much more in consonance with the generally accepted Jewish tradition than is my or my family's conception. You understand me, don't you?*

(The *Kaddish,* a sanctification of God, is recited daily by children in mourning for their parents at synagogue services for the period of one year. Traditionally, it is recited by sons. In default of male survivors, a stranger may act as substitute.)

August 13, 1936

To the Boy in Manchester who celebrated his religious coming of age by thought of his people in Germany and of the home of his people in Palestine.

My dear Boy,

We have not heard your name, we have heard only of an act of yours. But that knowledge of you is far greater than your name could have given us. It paints a picture for us

* From Marvin Lowenthal: "Henrietta Szold: Life & Letters." The Viking Press, New York, 1942.

of your mind and your soul. I should like to tell you what I, for one, learnt about you through your act. I learnt that you have no desire to multiply possessions; that you are alive to the needs of others; that you are touched to the quick by the indignities being put upon our people in Germany; that you realize how stunted must be the lives of boys like yourself who live in the Germany of today; that you not only feel their suffering, but you take the opportunity to relieve their suffering in so far as you can; that you know what is happening in the world and that the greatest thing that is happening to Jews is the opportunity of living in their old home and living there in accordance with their views and ideals cherished there many centuries; that all these thoughts and feelings are so strong in you as to make you utter them to others, your own companions, and so, I am sure, influence them to think the same thoughts and feel the same feelings as you think and feel.

We wanted to let you know that we appreciate your thoughts and share your feelings. Words seemed weak. So we who are taking care of the boys to whom your act of self-denial gave the great opportunity of their lives, to come out of darkness into light, put together for you some of the scenes in which your boys will be actors, in the land they are to build up.

We don't thank you; we only want to tell you that we are happy to have a co-worker like you in far-off Manchester.

Jerusalem, October 22, 1943
(Translated from the German)

Dear Miriam Henrietta Beyth!

Today you are one year old. I will no longer delay telling you how heartily I rejoice that you have come into our world. Many who know you and your dear parents rejoice in it. But my rejoicing is of a very special kind. Let me explain to you why it is unique.

You bear two names. The first, Miriam, belonged to your grandmother, your father's mother. He gave you her name, because he did not wish its memory lost. Through you, his beloved daughter, he will forever be reminded of his beloved mother. To this beloved name he has added mine. For that, I believe, he had a specific reason. From the first day of his entry into your fatherland, the land of our fathers, he was engaged in a beautiful, sacred, but most difficult task. In this task I also had a share, and it was the conquest of its difficulties that bound us together in close comradeship. It is because of this, perhaps, that my name symbolizes for him the work which he loves as a man loves his mother and his child. Just as one of your names will forever remind him of his beloved mother, so your second name will forever remind him of the beloved work of his heart and soul. Thus my name will live on through you, and therefore I greet you with a special rejoicing.

You will read this letter many years from now. You will be surprised that it was written in German, not in Hebrew. I am writing it in the language in which your father and I began our work in common, because at first he had little knowledge of Hebrew. The language will remind you, how in time of evil, his fate changed to good. It brought him and your mother into the land of our fathers, where he at once set himself the task of making it the eternal land of Jewish children, his own children and those of the many unhappy parents who were not privileged to come to the Land of Israel. That is his work—he himself will tell of it.

Dear Miriam Henrietta, may you always be as happy as you have made your parents by your arrival in this world!

(Miriam Henrietta will never hear the story from her father's lips. He was shot down December 25, 1947, while traveling on the Jerusalem—Tel Aviv road, in line of duty. See footnote, page 171.)

High Commissioners of Palestine

Sir Herbert Samuel, 1920–1925
Field Marshal Lord Plumer, 1925–1928
Sir John Chancellor, 1928–1931
Sir Arthur Grenfell Wauchope, 1931–1938
Sir Harold McMichael, 1938–1944
Field Marshal Lord Gort, 1944–1945
Sir Alan Gordon Cunningham, 1945–1948

Index

B-Szold, Henrietta cop.1
Zeitlin - Henrietta Szold
DISCARDED BY
FREE PUBLIC LIBRARY
NUTLEY, NEW JERSEY
FREE PUBLIC LIBRARY
NUTLEY 10, NEW JERSEY